BOOT CAMP

FOR CHRISTIAN WRITERS

A Handbook for Writers and Editors

L. EDWARD HAZELBAKER

BOOT CAMP
FOR CHRISTIAN WRITERS

A Handbook for Writers and Editors

L. EDWARD HAZELBAKER

BRIDGE
LOGOS

Newberry, FL 32669

Bridge-Logos
Newberry, FL 32669

Boot Camp for Christian Writers:
A Handbook for Writers and Editors
by L. Edward Hazelbaker

Printed in the United States of America.

Library of Congress Catalog Card Number: 2023935260

International Standard Book Number: 978-1-61036-412-6

The Author's Website:
TheWornKeyboard.com

Interior Layout and Cover Design:
Ashley Morgan
GraphicGardenLLC@gmail.com

What Others Are Saying

I've had the personal honor of working directly with this book's author as my Editor and Agent, and I'm unequivocally convinced that he is God's GIFT to every Christian writer. To have in your hands a manual that guides you step by step through the process of writing and publishing a book is one thing. To have a godly, seasoned minister, editor, mentor, and author walk alongside you until you are tipped over and poured out in your writing—unashamedly ignited to fulfill the Great Commission—is entirely another. This is L. Edward Hazelbaker! His passion for helping you turn your personal life story into a well-written manuscript that will bring hope to the world is as palpable as he is practical. You'll graduate from Boot Camp inspired and equipped to sit down at your keyboard and fulfill your calling as a Christian writer. The world is waiting to read what God created you to write! You NEED this book!

—JULIE SEALS, Hope Dealer
Co-founder, Her Hope Recovery Ministry

Boot Camp for Christian Writers immerses readers in a comprehensive practice designed to address the mind, body, and spirit simultaneously. From using Bible verses to teach correct syntax to offering specific steps for a prayerful approach, L. Edward Hazelbaker guides readers on a journey from idea to publication in a Christian context. In a clear, well-organized fashion, he addresses myriad aspects of the writing process, including some of the most important and daunting tasks a writer performs: revising and editing. By supplying anecdotes about his own writing, editing, and publishing experiences, Hazelbaker humanizes the text, so that writers feel cared for and watched over—a pleasant and welcome experience that epitomizes the concept of fellowship. A must-read for the Christian writer.

—**KENDALL KLYM,** PHD
Visiting Assistant Professor of English
Oklahoma State University

Finally, a boot camp for Christian writers in book form! L. Edward Hazelbaker is a blue-ribbon writer and editor, and now you get to glean from his extensive experience. From the big picture of a well-written, completed book, to the many details it takes to get there, Mr. Hazelbaker covers every aspect of writing—all from a solidly Christian perspective. *Boot Camp for Christian Writers* is a classic and will sit on your desk as a ready reference for years to come!

—**REVEREND DR. JAMIE MORGAN**
Mentor To Women In Ministry

Boot Camp for Christian Writers is both engaging and informative. L. Edward Hazelbaker has given to us an invaluable resource for aspiring writers as well as accomplished authors. His straightforward and detailed work gives us rules for writing effectively while providing clear explanations for why the rules apply. As a published author myself, I will be referring to this book often. It's a great tool and a refreshing reminder of how to fulfill our calling as Christian writers by serving our readers with excellence.

—**DONNA SPARKS,** Author, Prison Minister
Assemblies of God Evangelist

To personally know L. Edward Hazelbaker is to be encouraged by his insight and inspired by his commitments. It has been my enrichment to have experienced both from my friend, Lynn. *Boot Camp for Christian Writers* typifies who the author is and gives his readers the encouragement and education to pursue writing, both of which come from his wealth of experience. I highly recommend this resource to any aspiring novice, or even experienced author. As he wrote, "My goal is to help . . . " That goal has been fully accomplished in his inspirational and practical guide for writers.

—**DARREN PILCHER,** Senior Pastor
Spring Creek Assembly of God
Edmond, Oklahoma

As I read through the pages of *Boot Camp for Christian Writers*, I fondly recalled my experiences working with its author on two book projects. L. Edward's teaching-style of editing helped me understand the *why* behind his corrections to my manuscripts. I'm grateful for every kind correction, attaboy, and teachable moment. They were intentional investments he made in my life as a writer and as an individual. And that's in part what this book will be for you—an investment in your life to help you become the best writer you can be. Prepare to learn. Prepare to be challenged. And expect to improve. With his extensive experience—and a bit of humor—L. Edward Hazelbaker will quickly become a trusted voice in your writing endeavors.

—**DEBORAH STRICKLIN,** Assemblies of God Minister
Author, Founder, Deborah Stricklin Ministries

Dedication

To God be the glory, great things He hath done,
So loved He the world that He gave us His Son,
Who yielded His life an atonement for sin,
And opened the life-gate that all may go in.

Excerpt from *To God Be the Glory*
Lyrics by Fanny Jane Crosby

Acknowledgments

I, like most, have had many experiences and challenges in life. And I certainly acknowledge God as the only One who could have caused all of them to work together to prepare me for what He has allowed me to do today. As I attempt to help others, I can only hope to do that because HE is *my own* ever-present help.

Although they will need to read this from heaven's portal, my heartfelt appreciation goes out to two men whose friendship meant (and still means) so much to me—Rev. David A. Womack, my first editor and literary agent, and Dr. Robert B. Kamm, professor of English and former President of Oklahoma State University.

Then there are those authors who allowed me to partner with them in the development of their books. I won't call them all out by name. They know who they are. I appreciate them trusting me and allowing me to further hone my skills as an editor on their projects. I acknowledge them for the part they also had in the production of this book. We stand together. We learn together. We rejoice together.

And last but absolutely not least—in fact, right up there under God in my view—is my wife, Melveta, who has put up with me for over fifty-two years. I acknowledge her with pointed emphasis; for without her support, where would I be? Likely not here doing this. I'm grateful and without hesitation let my readers know her patience with me has been indispensable, and I love her.

Foreword

If you were going for a job interview, or indeed out on a date, you would want to look your best and be your best. You should have that attitude when presenting a manuscript to a publisher.

Publishers and editors want to be presented with the best possible final text you have to offer. But how do you make sure that's what they receive? This book is designed to answer that question.

It will mean some hard work, such as checking the correct punctuation and spelling in Bible references as well as the names of other people and places. And many manuscripts are simply too long. So it will take you pruning out what is not important and limiting yourself to the core message.

Editors don't expect perfection—they are there to help you. As the author of four books as well as being a publisher and editor, I understand the process and why it's necessary. L. Edward Hazelbaker makes these and many other things clear in his work.

So let's make your book the best it can be. And if you take on board all the help in the following chapters, you will certainly be a much better author.

—**ED HARDING,** Author, Editor and Director
Bridge-Logos Publishing

Table of Contents

Introduction

My first book, *The Pilgrim's Progress in Modern English*, was published in 1998. I updated *The Pilgrim's Progress* from its original 17th century English to the way we speak and write today.

With John Bunyan's classic work originally published in 1678—just sixty-seven years after the *King James Version* of the Bible was first published—you might imagine what kind of project that was. I worked five years to update the language of *The Pilgrim's Progress* and annotate the book without all the resources now available to writers at their fingertips through the internet.

After that, I updated two more of Bunyan's books and did some of my own original writing. But as I neared retirement age, my work shifted to mostly editing the work of others. Work on Bunyan's books definitely gave me some good preparation for that.

As I continued to provide editing services—with work ranging from minor editing to ghostwriting—I eventually started feeling like I wanted to help more writers. I came to understand there were a lot of people who had testimonies worth writing down and great inspirational thoughts to share, but many of them struggled with writing.

Many started well in their writing but didn't seem to know how to finish. Others were plagued with writing habits that did a disservice to the value of the content they held in their hearts. And still others (actually many others) just couldn't understand how to establish and maintain a smooth flow of thought without throwing statements into their work that drew the minds of readers off onto tangents.

I wanted to help more people write better, and I believed I could. I wanted to help them fulfill their callings as Christian writers, but I'm limited in how many I can help one on one. So I started thinking I should write a book to help Christian writers improve their work—a book to help people I'd never come to know in this lifetime.

My thoughts on that kept popping up from time to time, but I kept focusing my energy on other things. I kept busy, and I wasn't sure a larger audience would even be interested in what I had to share. But things started shifting in late January of 2023.

I found I had some time on my hands, and I spent a few weeks cooped up at home nursing along some poor health. In early January I had recently finished editing four books I'd been working on for several months, and even though I wasn't feeling well, I was enjoying a little time without pressure.

Then suddenly I heard a voice from heaven, saying, . . . No that definitely didn't happen. But for reasons I won't get into, it just seemed like I should start putting together an outline of what I would want to teach Christian writers if I were teaching a class.

So I got off my duff and . . . No, that actually didn't happen either. I opened up my laptop computer and placed it before me on my legs as I sat down *on* my duff in my recliner and began to write . . . er . . . type.

Three weeks later a simple outline had turned into 40,300 words, and that soon grew about 4,500 words larger and became the second draft of this book by the end of February.

In this book you'll find my approach in communicating to you is conversational, but beyond that, it's also sometimes pretty casual. And before jumping into making any recommendations on handling some basic grammatical issues, I discuss some things to build the groundwork for understanding and dealing with them.

Along the way I sprinkle in a few of my own experiences in life that I feel are relevant to things I discuss. I did that not only to better connect with you but also to encourage you in your work as a Christian writer.

Regardless of your education, regardless of your background, regardless of the mistakes you've made in life, and regardless of any pain and disappointment you may still have trouble overcoming, you will always be able to do what God has appointed you to do.

Your ability to do what God has called you to do is not limited—and I repeat, *is not limited*—by what you *think* of your abilities (or lack thereof). When God looks for people to work in His mission field called earth, He doesn't call people who can't do the work He gives them.

Despite your apprehensions and your weaknesses, you *can* do what God has called you to do, because He *has* already supplied and *will* continue to supply in the future exactly what you need to do it.

Count on it!

—LEH

— Chapter 1 —

Orientation to Boot Camp

IF YOU'VE BEEN called by God to write but don't know where to start, or even if you're already a writer and you're looking for help to become a better communicator, I wrote this book for you.

Welcome to Boot Camp!

This is where you face your challenges head on. This is where you come to grips with both your weaknesses and strengths. This is where you learn and hone your skills. And after finishing *Boot Camp* you'll be better prepared for your work as a Christian writer.

As you read my thoughts on writing, I'll do my best to provide you with helpful insight on how to become a better writer. And I'll definitely challenge you to continually take whatever you learn over the years about writing—or just about life—and put it to work. But first, let's go through *Boot Camp* orientation.

I want you to know what to expect from *Boot Camp for Christian Writers* before we start dealing with any of the actual business of writing. I want you to know what this book *is*, but first let me tell you what it is NOT.

This book is *not* intended to be an exhaustive study of the rules of grammar. It's *not* meant to be a style manual for writing or take the place of one. And it's *not* even intended to provide you with all you need to know to become a successful writer or communicator.

Stay with me here!

This book (and perhaps I should say, its author) makes no claim of being a premier authority on writing. And this book is *not* intended to take the place of a formal education. I will, however, throw in an editorial opinion here and say, while formal education is good, earning a diploma is not like gaining a magic key that opens the room where they store the best sellers list.

And as another part of your orientation to *Boot Camp*—just to set the scene for what's to come—I profess no identity as a lettered educator of English, a master of English literature, or a leading teacher of creative writing. I haven't pursued any of those stations in life.

I have some decent experience in writing. I'm a published author. And I'm a somewhat experienced editor and proofreader. But if you want to learn at the feet of a leading professor of English or be coached by a famous best-selling author, you'll need to look elsewhere. I'm not that person.

Now as far as what this book *is*, it's simply the outgrowth of one man's desire to help writers be better prepared for producing excellent work that's easily consumed, understood, welcomed, and appreciated by their readers. With that in mind, I believe this book has the potential to help many.

But to be clear, while many recommendations and guidelines I placed in this book have the potential of helping writers from many backgrounds and with other purposes in life, this book is unashamedly focused on helping

Christian writers fulfill their Great Commission callings to communicate to others the Good News. That should become clear as you continue reading.

More About This Book

This Book's Goal

It'll be great if I can give you a spiritual boost along the way—I'd like to do that—but the primary goal of this book is simple. My goal is to *help* you become a better writer. Did you see my emphasis is on the word "help"?

There's no way for me or anyone else to "make" you a better writer. God intends for all Christian writers to become better over time as we gain experience, but we all have our own parts to play in applying ourselves to do those things that will lead to our success as communicators of the gospel.

Like so many other things in life, in order to become better at writing, we must first *want* to get better. But even *wanting* to get better is just the beginning of our progress toward being able to produce works of excellence.

> We'll never become better at anything by only expressing our desire. That desire must lead to action.

If we share in the vision of becoming better writers and producing good work, we should also share in our determination to not only take every opportunity to learn but also apply what we learn. And that's the launching pad for me telling you that if you haven't already started writing, you need to start now.

The sooner you start doing what God's called you to do, the sooner you'll learn to do it better. Doing and learning at the same time is the best way to build skills.

So one of my goals with this book is to encourage you to start writing (if you haven't already started) and keep writing. Don't wait until you think you possess all the knowledge you need before you start doing the work. And once you start, keep writing to gain more experience, knowledge, and confidence.

You see, learning or memorizing facts, rules, and principles is fine, but when we actually learn by doing, that's when things really start making sense. Our potential to master principles of good writing is tremendously enhanced when we put them into practice.

A good many people have a higher IQ and better education than I have. And there are a good many people with better memories. When it comes to needing someone to quickly pull things out of memory and regurgitate facts, rules, and principles to explain all the detailed rules of grammar and why things should be done a certain way, I'm not at the top of the list of people to call.

"Umm, let me get back to you on that," I say as I look for where I put my copy of *The Chicago Manual of Style*.

I'm not the one to write a dictionary or style manual. But I'm the one to use them. I may not be the one to teach a theory. But I'm the one to put it to the test. I'm not the one to remember all the proper terms used when explaining why something is done. But I'm the one to do it. And why?

Because I've learned by doing, and experience has taught me that method works.

People express to me their reluctance to step out and do what they want to do—or what God has called them to do (and sometimes there's no difference). They talk about not knowing how to start and how they don't have the experience they feel they need. That's real life. I understand that.

God's always asking us to go beyond our abilities! Go figure. And I have compassion for their predicament. But here's what I tell them:

> "I've never done anything until
> I did it for the first time."

To be clear, I'm not saying you should take on any task without putting some effort toward first familiarizing yourself with the work before you. Before building something for the first time, I look into how others have done it; I learn what I can about their processes and the tools required for the job.

I do some research and ask questions. I look up standards and requirements that should be followed. But the knowledge I gain through all of those exercises never results in a completed project until I pick up the tools and go to work.

Further, once that first project is completed—even if I made a lot of mistakes that a seasoned builder would not have made—I gained a mountain of knowledge through my experience of *doing* the work compared to the molehill of information I had when I started.

Neither I nor my work is perfect. And I'll leave it to you to determine your own level of perfection. But we serve a perfect God, and I know He intends to use and improve on whatever we have to give Him. If we give Him what we have, He will give us more. That's a principle that even works in giving to God our time, our efforts, and what skills we have to give Him.

My hope is that what I've done with this book will in some way help you as we both give God what we have and allow Him to improve and enable our walks and our work to point others to Him and HIS glory!

This Book's Approach

I do my best in this book to share with you some knowledge without getting any more technical than necessary. As you continue reading, I hope you'll see I'm not interested in sharing a lot of things to impress the masses. Whatever I'm sharing, I'm sharing with you—*you*—one person who desires to follow God and write for Him.

Basically, I hope you'll see this book as an extension of my heart to serve you and others who are doing their best to serve God with the various talents and capabilities God has given to each of us.

This is my attempt to partner with you for your benefit and that of the Kingdom. And especially today, with the ease of worldwide communications all around us, we don't need to live nearby to be able to partner with others in fulfilling the Great Commission. As we partner with one another and help each other prosper in our callings, we're strengthened together regardless of the physical distance that separates us.

A person standing alone can be attacked and defeated, but two can stand back-to-back and conquer. Three are even better, for a triple-braided cord is not easily broken.
(Ecclesiastes 4:12)

It's in the spirit of forming a partnership with you in ministry that I invite you to read on and see if together we can take some significant strides toward doing our parts in answering God's call to share the Good News with the world.

— Chapter 2 —

Learning from the Beginning

IN ORDER TO have a meaningful partnership, I need to give you a little information on my background. You'll need to get to know me on at least some personal level in order for you to know where I'm coming from, fully grasp my approach to writing, and understand my attempts to encourage you.

Then after you get to know me a little—and before I start dealing with any details on the mechanics of writing—I'll move on in the following chapters to discuss several topics relevant to understanding the business, or ministry, of Christian writing. I want to use the early chapters as a foundation upon which to build what follows.

I recommend you first read this book from top to bottom in the order I'm presenting it. Then later you can use the book's table of contents to allow you to use the book more as a reference when dealing with specific issues.

My Background

I was born in 1952 to parents who moved to California from Oklahoma during the Second World War. My mother received her lifetime teaching certificate from Central State Teacher's College in Edmond, Oklahoma, in 1931. My mother used that teaching certificate in California when she and the woman senior pastor of our church—Harbor City Foursquare Church—opened up a private school in 1948.

Harbor City Christian School—in a suburb of South Los Angeles—opened with my mother as the only teacher. And she taught nine students on multiple grade levels during the first year the school was in operation. It was the example of a one-room schoolhouse in the big city.

The school soon grew larger, though, and in time it became a K–12 school with the church having to build new facilities to house all the classes.

I attended that school from kindergarten through most of the seventh grade, when in the early spring of 1965 my parents moved back to Oklahoma with me, their youngest of five children. When we moved from Harbor City, the school my mother started with nine students had grown to a student body of around 600.

My mother was still teaching in the school when we moved. She taught all those years because that was her calling, and it allowed my parents to have enough money to finance the education of their five children in the private school she started. I credit my mother and my early education for instilling within me a desire to learn.

But of course, I give God the credit for anything of value that I've personally done in my life. I freely admit that without Him I could have done none of it.

Like others, I've made my fair share of mistakes during my lifetime, but I've never been forsaken by God. And for whatever reason He's had for doing so, the Lord has enabled me to accomplish more in life than I would have thought possible—and definitely much more than I deserve.

The Pilgrimage

There was a particular book that impressed me as a young person. It was a book written and first published in 1678 by a non-conformist preacher in England by the name of John Bunyan. He wrote several books, but his most popular was that unique and celebrated allegory—*The Pilgrim's Progress: From this World To That Which Is To Come.*

There was a time when one could find a copy of *The Pilgrim's Progress* in the libraries of nearly all Christian families in America who had collections of books. And *The Pilgrim's Progress* was required reading in all schools that had any serious interest in teaching English Literature— yes, in *public* schools across the nation. And to this day it's been said that since Bunyan first published *The Pilgrim's Progress*, only the Bible has had better historic sales among all of English Literature.

As an adult with three children, I decided it would be good to divide up some family time into several sessions and read the book to my children. So my wife and I gathered the children before us in the living room one day, and I began to read. But I hadn't gone far into my reading until I could tell by the looks in my children's eyes they were having trouble with it.

I gave up that effort shortly thereafter. Common English written in the 1600s is even harder to deal with than the proper English of the King James Version of the Bible. It saddened me, and I began thinking that someone should take that marvelous book and translate it into more modern English in its entirety so people today and tomorrow could continue to gain from it.

To make a long story shorter, *The Pilgrim's Progress in Modern English*—my first book—was published by Bridge-Logos Publishers in 1998 to take its place among their Pure Gold Classics series of updated classic Christian literature.

Years before it was published, the feeling had come to me and never left me that I should update the language myself even if only my own children could benefit from it. And after a few years, I finally began what turned into a five-year project of updating the language and structure of *The Pilgrim's Progress* to make it palatable and appealing for today's and tomorrow's readers.

And while doing that work, I also decided to fully annotate the book, and that made the work even more challenging than it would have otherwise been. After those five years of labor, I still remember the feeling of accomplishment I had when I opened a package sent to me containing the very first copy of *The Pilgrim's Progress in Modern English* that rolled off the press.

After experiencing that, you might imagine why I look forward to hearing the responses of the authors I help when they receive their books for the first time. And if you've never experienced that, I look forward to the time when you do.

Bunyan himself added to *The Pilgrim's Progress* approximately 500 annotations consisting of short comments and Scripture references. When I finished my work of further annotating the book, I had added well over 800 additional annotations, which included approximately 66 direct Scripture quotations used in the narrative by Bunyan but not annotated by him.

Needless to say, I had never taken on a task like that, and after those years of work, I found I had learned a lot about writing and editing. I eventually followed that book with the updates of two more of John Bunyan's books—*Grace Abounding* and *The Holy War*.

You may feel like what God has called you to do is too big for you. Many Christians who are called into action by God feel that way. You're not alone. I've dealt with feelings like that. But there comes a time when we all must rise up and cast feelings aside.

Now only because I want to encourage you further to trust God by accepting big challenges that He places before you, I'm sharing here a snippet of the Foreword to *The Pilgrim's Progress in Modern English* as written by Dr. Robert B. Kamm, President Emeritus of Oklahoma State University, and former Professor of English.

Noting that Bible scholars and translators were producing more readable translations of the Bible to reach more people of all age groups and nationalities, other translators went to work to make *The Pilgrim's Progress* more readable. Recently, L. Edward Hazelbaker, a former brick mason and now a computer professional in Architectural and Engineering Design at Oklahoma State University, committed himself to translating the original book into modern English without losing the flavor and the power of John Bunyan's original volume. Although not a "lettered man" (in his own words), Mr. Hazelbaker may well be an ideal person to translate John Bunyan's work, in that Bunyan, too, was somewhat of a craftsman and a man of limited formal education. Further, Hazelbaker, an Assemblies of God minister, has other things in common with the Puritan preacher, John Bunyan. (At this point, it's interesting to note that Jesus, too, was a craftsman and was considered by many as "unlettered"!)

As a writer, I benefitted from the efforts of some wonderful mentors, such as Dr. Kamm and the editors who took the time to explain their edits to me when they proofed my work. Those men became my mentors as they yielded themselves to God when they were called to *help* me.

Learning by doing seems to be *my forte*, and I've seen that process happening throughout my life in more than just writing. Because of my willingness to learn by doing—and specifically here in context with writing—in time I was able to use what I learned through my work of updating Bunyan's books to not only write better but also begin proofing and editing a number of books for other Christian authors.

Now I've taken on another project because it weighed on my mind for a long time—this book.

I know by experience that there are many capable followers of Christ who have a great passion for participating in the Great Commission. I know they're driven by the Spirit and have some great thoughts to share with others.

I know God wants to use them. But when it comes to taking their thoughts and putting them down on paper, I also know many of them struggle. I have a desire to *help* them by sharing some basic things that will contribute to them finishing the jobs God has called them to do.

This book is the culmination of my effort to take my desire to do that and put it to work.

> If you gain nothing else from the rest of this book, I hope you gain the knowledge and confidence that you don't have to be the world's idea of a *somebody* to accomplish the *something* God has for you to do.

— Chapter 3 —

Who We Are
as Writers

LIKE IT OR NOT, the quality of our work (what we produce) cannot be separated from who we are, and that's because who we are is largely *defined* by what we do. And as I consider that, I'm thinking James, the brother of Jesus,[1] addressed that general concept pretty well when he wrote about understanding biblical faith.

> But do you want to know, O foolish man, that faith without works is dead? (James 2:20 NKJV)

At the root of the faith that leads to Salvation is faith that leads to *action*. And to James, it was apparent that if there is no evidence of action on someone's part—action that can be seen to testify to the reality of that person's faith—there is no faith.

In taking his stand, James didn't pull out of the sky some super-spiritual concept when dealing with confusion in people's minds about how faith exists and how it's defined. All James did was apply some logic.

---

[1]   Mary and Joseph had other children in their family. James was the half-brother of Jesus since the Holy Spirit was Jesus' father (Matthew 1:18). Jesus also had sisters (Matthew 13:55–56).

If something exists (and we actually know about it), it's known in large part by what it does. Electrons and protons existed long before we knew about them, but we came to know about them only when we developed the capability of observing what they do.

So this isn't even a biblical concept. It just makes sense. Beyond James having spiritual insight, he was a sensible realist.

This is what a realist knows: Shoddy work is produced by shoddy workmen. Excellent work is produced by excellent tradesmen. The quality of work is a reflection of the quality of the worker.

Good grapes are produced on good vines. Cars that don't break down every time you turn around are manufactured in good plants by good workers using good parts following good procedures and plans drawn up by good engineers and designers employed by good administrators of good companies. (Whew! That was a mouthful.)

> What we produce, regardless of what we're talking about, is in one way or another a reflection on us. And as writers, what we produce is writing.

Since we're revealed to others by our work, it makes sense for us to at least consider at some point who we are (and what makes us who we are) as we answer God's call and launch ourselves into the work of becoming accomplished Christian writers.

That's what you want to be, right? And that's definitely what I want to help you become.

To be able to be the best we can be *for* Christ, we must also do our best to know Him and His intentions for us. And we'll discover more about that as we learn more about His work on earth. And by actually doing that, we'll begin coming to know more about ourselves.

One step leads to another. And then by both coming to know God and coming to know ourselves, we'll be brought into the ideal position for the Holy Spirit to accomplish God's will in us—His will to work *in* us and *through* our writing.

Knowing God is a larger subject than I would like to tackle in this book. So much could be said. So many books have been and could still be written on that subject. So for the purpose of this book, we'll stay focused on defining and knowing *us*. And to do that, I'll speak about what God has already revealed about both who we are and who we are not.

Who We Are

I think it's a good idea for us to get a good, realistic handle on who or what we are in the world before we set out to do the task set before us. We need to understand ourselves. It's even Scriptural to examine our own actions (1 Corinthians 11:31). It's something we should do.

Before we begin our task, we should consider what we already know and what we still need to learn. And in our work as writers, it's important that we maintain a pretty firm grip on reality. That will help us stay centered in our relationships with God and enable us to better relate to readers in humility (more on this to come).

In Christian writing, we're normally involved in either witnessing or teaching. We witness to others and tell them what God has done for us, or in us, by writing down our personal testimonies. And when we teach, we explain the truths of the Bible and address in writing the many, many issues of life. We expound on what God has revealed to mankind and what He's done in and through others over the course of history.

Regardless of whether we're witnessing or teaching from Scripture (and many times it's both), when we write we generally do it to enlighten, encourage, or inspire our readers. And through that, we hope to provide an opportunity for the Holy Spirit to minister to the reader in any way God sees fit.

We do our part, and God does His part. But I'm convinced we'll never be able to do our part the way God would have us do it if we lose sight of what place we have in fulfilling the Great Commission through writing.

God's Gift to the World (service)

To become and be everything God wants us to be, we need to realize that God wants to actually *give us* to others as His gift. Hang on to that thought for a moment.

Yes, God saves us for our own benefit. He wants our future to be filled with His blessings—with the arms of the Father firmly wrapped around us in true familial relationship. But His plans for us as members of His family go far beyond that.

Our spiritual union with the Father made possible through the sacrifice of Jesus for our sins is the beginning of a new life—a new existence. And as we continue to discover more about our heavenly Father's desires and plans for us, the things we learn usher in a clearer and more vibrant realization of our purpose (at least it should).

As followers of Christ, we were saved from destruction for our good, but we were also saved to benefit those around us with our lives and good works. And we do that as we return to God the gifts He gives to us by sharing them with others.

God has always given gifts to mankind, and one of the most important of those gifts is His own presence as He shares and demonstrates His love and concern for people through His children. You may not have considered this, but *you* are intended to be a gift from God. And that's because you've been chosen to become His *vessel of blessing.*

As His vessel of blessing, God places within you the gifts that will not simply be a blessing to you (and they will) but also be a blessing to others.

> God wants you as a Christian writer
> to be tipped over and poured out
> through your writing. And when you, as
> God's gift to others, are poured
> out on them, that's called *service.*

As long as we keep our heads on straight, it's not wrong for us to view ourselves as a gift from God, because that's what God intends for us to be. And to keep our heads properly screwed on, all we need to do is remember that in addition to being God's gifts, we're also God's servants.

We can claim to be—and indeed are—God's gifts, as He intends, only as we reflect the gift God gave to the world when Jesus came to live among us. And I have more to say about that in the next section.

Who We Are Not

One of the things I've noticed in life is that what things *are* is defined just as much by what they *are not.* "White" is really what we know it to be because it's not "black." We could never fully appreciate the identity or the quality of "white" if we could never compare it to its opposite. So to be all God wants and aims for us *to be*, we must maintain a firm grip on who God wants us *not to be*.

God's Gift to the World (attitude)

As I've mentioned, I have some decent experience in both writing and editing. At my age I also have some experience in a lot of other things I won't take the time to mention. And even if all of those things on the surface don't seem to be directly related, I believe God has used the accumulation of all my experiences to lead me to what I'm doing right now in life.

My point is, I've learned things through all my experiences, and all those experiences have worked together for my benefit—to prepare me for *now*. And I have every confidence the same process will continue until I take my last breath on earth. Why? Because it's Scriptural.

> *And we know that God causes everything to work together for the good of those who love God and are called according to **his purpose for them**.*
>
> (Romans 8:28 [emphasis mine])

Note the emphasis on the reason for God working things together. Now that I've drawn your attention to that, I also confess that I'm a retired minister, and because of it, from time to time I can shift into *preacher mode*. And I'm doing that right now.

I've already said that you, as a Christian writer, are God's gift to others. And by extension, therefore, you are God's gift to the world. I believe that, and I've already explained it in at least a rudimentary way. But I hope to make it abundantly clear that you're God's gift to the world *as a servant.*

> You and I are gifts to the world
> because we bear within us and serve
> to the world what it needs most
> —God's presence and blessings.

Here it comes!

I admonish you not to begin viewing yourself as God's gift to the world in *attitude*. For if you do, that's where you'll surely stumble. Stay on top of your attitude at all times, or you'll falter and fail in your ability to walk closely with God and be all God wants you to be as a Christian writer.

When Jesus walked on the earth He could have done or had anything He wanted. He could have ascended the throne of ultimate power in the world and enslaved all the nations. He could have demanded respect from the leaders of the world. He could have had all the rulers of earth bow before Him and yield their crowns to Him even if they didn't want to do it.

Jesus could have waved His hand without speaking a word and destroyed the Roman Empire. Within His spirit was the power of the Universe. All knowledge and all wisdom resided within Him in the flesh. He could have written **all** the books and demanded the whole earth's population to acknowledge His understanding of the secrets of the Universe. But what did He do?

He washed His disciples' feet.[2]

---

2   John 13:1–17.

I hope you excel in writing for the Kingdom. But as a minister of the Word I caution you to never view yourself any more highly than you should. I hope you write a book that sells at least a million copies. But I also pray that when you do, you'll still be filled with the same humility that resided in Christ.

Neither of us is God's gift to the world if that's our attitude. We always need to keep the gift we *are* in context with how God views us—in context with His call and plan for us—and not how the flesh would tempt us to view ourselves.

If you stray into the realm of the flesh's tendency to get a big head or entertain a feeling of superiority from wealth, influence, notoriety, or success (or from anything else for that matter), I pray that God's Spirit will come to you, correct you, and lead you back into the path of service and humility He has planned for your life.

Your greatest success as a Christian writer and your eternal reward will depend on that.

— Chapter 4 —

Writing vs. Speaking

NOW WE'RE BEGINNING to move from mere background to deal with understanding some dynamics of communicating in writing. For starters, I'll address the definite differences between verbal and written communication. And since so many Christian *writers* were first Christian *speakers*, their abilities to make the transition from speaking to writing may be challenging.

Basic Differences

I was reminded some time back that "93% of communication is in body language, facial expressions, and voice tone." My response to that reminder was, "And it's unfortunate that writers must produce effective and clear communications for their readers without all three of them."

As a Christian writer—any writer for that matter—you can't motion with your hands to provide animation to your words. You can't move around on a platform to maintain the focus and attention of your audience. You can't grimace, smile, shake your head, or raise your eyebrows as a signal to let your audience know how you feel about what you just said. And you can't raise or lower your voice to add emphasis.

You can't use any movement of your body; you can't use any facial expression, and you can't use any intonation of your voice to signal either sarcasm or seriousness to your readers. All you have are words and your use of them—period!

That's a big difference, and searing this into your memory will help you.

Many people who speak well before a live audience—yes, people like preachers—can have trouble writing as well as they speak. Many listeners captivated by some speakers' deliveries will not be impressed at all with their writing skills. And there are plenty of good writers who capture the interest of readers but are not good at public speaking.

Delivering thoughts and ideas in public speaking and delivering those same thoughts and ideas in writing are two separate forms of communication. And only a limited number of people who do one of them well will be able to do both of them equally well.

> For many writers, acknowledging and remembering the differences in dynamics between speaking and writing is going to be the very first key to learning how to communicate to readers successfully.

To get our points across in writing, we need to understand and accept that we have at our disposal only written words, the organization of those words in phrases and sentences, and some limited tools of providing emphasis to words, phrases, and sentences.

Methodical Development

Regardless of whether we're *speaking* or *writing* to a group of people, it's important to make our delivery in a methodical and organized way. At the top of any organized speech, sermon, article, or book will always be the central thought, or theme. And hopefully the central thought is revealed in one way or another by the message's title.

The central thought encapsulates the overarching theme revealed within the message. And to be successful, everything spoken or written to become part of that message's delivery should relate in some way to addressing that overarching theme.

Regardless of how many points there are in what speakers or writers deliver to their audiences, to be effective they must all serve to lead the audience to accept and understand the primary message or help define it.

In a speech or spoken sermon, it's well accepted that only a small number of main points should be made while delivering the message. After all, *listeners* can only take in so many points through one ear before they begin leaking out of the other.

But many more points can be made in writing. Readers aren't tied down like people sitting in a room listening to a speech or sermon. Readers can find a place to stop reading, mark their place, lay down the book, and take it up later.

Writers aren't confined to delivering a message that can fit into a mere thirty or forty-five-minute time frame. Writers can develop a huge book that takes a month to read (assuming it's good enough for the reader to give it that much time).

Then as for organizing the main points included in a book, those points are generally organized into chapters. I suppose that's pretty much a given understood by just about everyone. But perhaps not so obvious is that when narrating a story—whether it be fiction or telling your life story for a testimony—the writer needs to organize chapters in basic chronological order.

And in any writing, the chapters should be organized in a way that each chapter builds on the truth or content of the previous chapter—or in a way that will at least make sense to the reader leading up to the final statements made to end the book.

As for bringing a book to an end with a strong final chapter, you wouldn't think a writer would need to be reminded that the end of the book should contain an appealing and effective closing that emphasizes the completion of dealing with the theme of the book. But that's sometimes necessary.

Writers will sometimes wander off on a line of thought and get so wrapped up and lost in it that they fail to return to the main thought and bring it to a close in context with the book's theme. And one thing you can count on, if writers are prone to do that at the end of the book, they're probably doing that at the end of chapters too.

That's enough said on that for the time being.

Interjections and Tangents

While writers have the advantage of being able to take up a lot more of the audience's time while developing and delivering a message, the writer is at a disadvantage in another way. Writers don't have the privilege to inadvertently interject stray thoughts into their deliveries or lead their readers' minds off on a tangent without paying a serious price.

Of critical importance for writers is the need to develop and maintain a smooth flow of thought throughout their manuscripts.

> To be effective, and to gain and maintain the respect of readers, writers must stay on point at all times. They must not allow stray thoughts to derail their efforts.

The writer must stay focused and be disciplined enough to recognize when a statement may lead the reader off topic and away from the author's point. It can be difficult to bring the reader's mind back into the proper flow of thought if the reader's mind drifts off on a tangent.

When proofing the manuscript, if writers don't catch what could and probably will lead readers' minds off topic —and fix it—the readers are left to find their own way back. And if there are enough troubling spots in a book where readers' minds are tossed back and forth from one thought or one topic to another, readers can get so frustrated with the writer that they put the book down before completing it—never to pick it back up.

To delve deeper into the importance of maintaining a smooth *flow of thought* in writing, look to Chapter 12.

Getting Away With It

While speakers may be disadvantaged by time constraints and the attention spans of their audiences, they also have some advantages over writers. And those advantages are significant. In fact, they're so significant that writers should never forget about them.

When it comes to maintaining a proper flow of thought throughout their deliveries, speakers have a huge advantage over writers when it comes to introducing interjections and tangents into their messages.

Speakers can get away with saying things that lead the thoughts of their listeners off topic in ways that writers can't. And that's due to a number of factors. One of them is simply the proximity of the audience to the speaker.

Proximity of the Audience

When a speaker stands before and addresses a group of people sitting in a room—regardless of the size of the room or crowd—the group of people sitting before the speaker is a captive audience. Sure, people can get up and leave if they like, but that isn't going to happen much, because it would cause most people leaving to become objects of attention and possibly cause them embarrassment.

The Focus of Attention

The speaker is in front of the audience. Normally the speaker will be standing, and the audience will be sitting. The speaker is the focus of attention. And even if something or someone draws the attention of a listener away from the speaker for a moment (including a stray thought), the attention will soon return to the speaker.

Overcoming Distraction

Any normal distraction that's introduced when a group of people are gathered in an auditorium is minimized by the fact that the speaker is the only one who actually has the formal right to be heard. And in most instances, if there's not a huge, noisy distraction taking place among the assembly, the speaker will be both heard and watched by those in the audience unless people close their eyes and put their fingers in their ears. (And depending on the volume of the PA system, that won't even work.)

Expectations

Believe it or not, most people sitting in an audience *expect* the speaker to both make mistakes and lead them off on tangents. They expect speakers to stumble over or forget words. And they aren't surprised at all when a speaker leaves his or her outline and makes an interjection of a thought that leads away from the main focus. In fact, they may even be amused by it.

Even if the speaker doesn't give the audience a clear signal by body language, facial expression, or tone of voice that the interjection was intentional, their minds will quickly return to the intended flow of thought and easily leave the interjection behind (perhaps tucking it away for later) as they catch back up with the speaker's line of thought.

Personal Dedication

In a church setting, the people in the audience likely have a personal interest in attending that goes beyond the specific message being delivered. If a speaker occasionally has a less-than-powerful message to share, or if a speaker occasionally has a difficult time staying on point and impressing the audience with delivery, the listeners are normally not easily dissuaded from continuing their dedication to either the church or the speaker. Most of the time those in the audience give the speaker plenty of chances to keep their confidence.

Speaker Insight

In addition to the way visual or aural dynamics affect the audience's ability to receive the message, speakers are also in a position to react to the audience in ways impossible for writers.

Members of an audience will combine what they hear with what they see to understand what the speaker is delivering to them. And in a similar manner the speaker will also receive clues from the audience.

Speakers with any experience at all will know when they're connecting with listeners. If the listeners become confused or begin questioning the direction a speaker's delivery is going, the speaker will pick up on that from the visual cues unintentionally provided by the audience.

Based on those types of clues, speakers have the opportunity to respond with statements like, "I'm not sure where that came from," or, "But getting back on topic . . . ," or, "You can just have that for no charge." Or they can come back with any number of other witty responses to make the listeners laugh or disregard a statement, leave it behind, and get back on track with the speaker.

Writers—that is, WE—have none of those advantages! Too bad, I guess we'll just have to learn how to deal with it and adjust our deliveries.

Or not . . . It's really up to us.

— Chapter 5 —

Serving Your Readership

HAVING ESTABLISHED a basic foundation built out of a combination of understanding our own unique positions as writers and the dynamics we're left to deal with, we now begin our manuscript. Of course I realize you may have already started writing. But regardless, even if you've already completed your manuscript, before you proof and finish your work it's a good idea to sit down and think about your readership one more time.

To whom are you writing? Who do you expect to have as your readers? Are they really going to get what you're writing?

> You'll be able to write for your readers' understanding and connect with them only after you actually know your readership.

Identifying Your Readership

Regardless of whether your work is to be delivered by speaking or by writing, there's nothing wrong with delivering what God gives you to a broad range of listeners or readers as long as that's your intended audience. But if you're writing for that broad range, you need to write in a style and use words and sentence structures that at least the majority of readers will understand and appreciate.

When addressing a broad, general audience, if you write using terms and methods familiar only to those in higher education, or use a style comfortable to only those accustomed to reading theses on theology, you'll likely lose a lot of less-educated readers. You'll also likely lose the interest of many who are lost, many of the Christian laity, and perhaps even some teachers in the Church. (I'm not trying to be tacky here.)

On the other hand—at the other end of the spectrum—if you communicate only in ways less-educated readers can understand, many who are lost but still better educated may be offended by being fed a shallow message. So the importance of finding a balance in how you write can't be dismissed if you're going to be a successful communicator.

Here are some of Paul's words to the Corinthians that are part of a larger remark about how he intentionally made himself to be a servant to all people even though he was a free man.

> *When I am with those who are weak, I share their weakness, for I want to bring the weak to Christ. Yes, I try to find common ground with everyone, doing everything I can to save some. I do everything to spread the Good News and share in its blessings.*
>
> (1 Corinthians 9:22–23)

Prior to writing these words, Paul spoke of how he identified with Jews when he was with Jews and identified with Gentiles when he was with Gentiles. He was talking about identifying *with* his audience (knowing how to approach them) so he could share the gospel with them on their level.

Paul knew it was important to know his audience and know how to deal with them. And it's also important for us to know our readership and know how to write *for* them if we're going to successfully communicate *with* them.

Now just in case someone could misunderstand my views, I see nothing wrong with writing to appeal to or satisfy theologians. But if that's your goal, you just need to be aware that your readership will be relatively small compared to a more general audience. If that's your target audience, write for them.

Even focusing on writing primarily for preachers— evangelists and pastors—can limit your pool of potential readers. And if your work is primarily aimed at having a readership of only pastors, the number of readers is even smaller than *preachers*. But if that's your purpose, if that's the readership the Lord wants you to address, then write to that audience. And write in a way that will best appeal to them.

If however you plan to write for the edification of all believers, write in a way that makes your goal clear to all—or at least to the majority of them. Use methods, terminology, and style that a broad array of people will easily be able to consume and appreciate.

Writing for the Reader

Writing for your readership in style, words, and complexity is covered above. And now I turn your attention to something else related to satisfying the needs of your audience.

In this tiny section I actually bring up a HUGE issue for you to think about. It's the fact that we're writing *for* our readers and not *for* ourselves.

> If you're writing to satisfy yourself,
> there's no need to write at all.

— Chapter 6 —

Steps to Producing a Good Manuscript

BELOW I PROVIDE you with a suggested list of steps to follow in order to increase your chances of producing a good manuscript. I feel that following these steps is useful in the process. But regardless of whether or not you find them useful, at least the steps are useful to me right now. They allow me to make some important points.

1. Prayerfully approach your work.

    I don't spend much time in this book writing about the part prayer plays in Great Commission writing. This book isn't about prayer. My main focus must be on addressing many other things. Regardless of the direction your calling leads you, my assumption has to be that you already know about the importance of prayer. (And I assume episodes of writer's block will drive at least some of you to your knees, anyway.)

    But I'll add something short and sweet here. If prayer is an important component in preparing you to stand before a live audience and deliver a message from God, it stands to reason that it's equally important when developing a book with a message from God. In fact, it can be even more important, because the words you write may affect more people for much longer than you can imagine.

2. Begin without expecting perfection.

Once you decide what you want to write about, perhaps the best way to get started is just to get started. Start writing down your thoughts about what you want to tell your audience. And although I'll sometimes start by developing an outline listing a theme, topics, and points, that doesn't mean a written outline is always required. But if you don't have an outline of some sort even in your mind, putting one on paper isn't a bad idea.

As you write, it will become clearer to you how to add to and organize your work. More thoughts will come to you as you write, and your work will expand. Just make sure you maintain reasonable expectations. Know up front that nobody produces polished work with a first draft, or second draft, or third draft . . . You get the idea.

3. Do something else.

Once you finish a first draft (and it may be the first draft of only one chapter), you need to set your work aside for a while and do something else. And you may need to set it aside for a day or so. Don't wear yourself out. Everyone needs a break. And writers need to get away from their pen and paper—or away from their keyboards—to give their minds and eyes a rest.

4. Read and edit it.

When you return to your work after you've been away from it for a period of time, you'll be able to see it with fresher eyes. And don't be surprised when you read it with fresher eyes if you see right away some problems you need to address and the need to clarify or add more material.

Also, if you thought your work was great when you first wrote it and now think it's pretty bad, you won't be the first to experience that. It's actually pretty common. Writers will sometimes feel uniquely inspired and write like crazy—thinking words of eloquence are flowing out of their minds like a gusher—only to later pick up what they wrote and think, "Where did that come from?"

Going back to your work to read and edit it with reasonable expectations is just part of the necessary processes employed by accomplished writers.

5. Do something else.

   After you've gone through another writing and editing session, get away from your work once again. Clear your mind. Think about something else for a while.

6. Read and edit it.

   Pick up your work again and see what needs to be improved. Continue to add to it the things that will enlarge and give substance to your thoughts and add more value to the work for the reader.

7. Don't hesitate to rewrite or prune the work.

   After laboring long hours and putting great effort into your writing you may see the need to reorganize your thoughts. Don't hesitate to do that. You may see passages that you once felt were important but now suddenly appear as extra baggage and no longer necessary. Prune them out.

You may even see content that has become counterproductive to reaching your goals. Don't hesitate to get rid of it. Rewrite for clarity. Prune away dead wood to make more room for the branches bearing fruit.

8. Start over if necessary.

Are you unsatisfied with how your work is turning out? Did you make a wrong turn? Is it becoming something you didn't mean it to be? Sometimes we can lose control of a narrative. Sometimes we can find ourselves getting distracted and starting to chase rainbows.

Sometimes we need to re-center our efforts. And sometimes we just need to start over. Clearly that can be disappointing. But just think, at that point you have some experience addressing the theme of your work. You're now in a better position to keep your thoughts in alignment with your intentions.

9. Proof it for excellence.

I tell authors that proofing and editing a manuscript should never end until the typeset copy of the book has been sent to the printer. If I'm involved in a writing project, I proof a manuscript at every stage. I proof it a final time before it's sent to a publisher for review. Assuming it's accepted for publishing, I proof it again before I send it to the publisher for copyediting. I then proof it after it's returned from the publisher's copyeditor, and I proof it yet again after it's typeset.

But even with all that proofing, it's not all that uncommon to read the published book later and find an error that slipped by everyone on the way to the printer. It's also not uncommon to identify things that, while written logically and clearly, could still be further improved. Those are things that can possibly be corrected in a second or third printing if the book is popular and sells well.

10. Have your work edited.

My advice to all who have a calling to write is to refuse to be satisfied with work just because it has improved to the point that it pleases them. We haven't done our best work if we've produced something that just satisfies us. Our work needs to satisfy our readers. And an experienced editor is in the best position to examine our work to see how it comes across to others.

The editor doesn't live in our minds, so the accomplished editor is better able to receive our words like other readers. Even the most successful writers have editors, and *Boot Camp* continues as the next chapter expands on the importance and process of being edited.

— Chapter 7 —

Even Editors
Need Editors

THE TITLE OF this chapter is a saying given to me by my own editor many years ago. Now with years of experience of my own in both writing and editing, I understand its truth more than ever, and I share it with the authors I help.

In this chapter I'll attempt to clarify what editors are and why people you know who are not experienced editors may not provide you with the services you need to properly evaluate your writing and consult with you to make your work the best it can be.

About Editors

Editors are people whose experience qualifies them to read with a critical eye and identify problems in writing. And it's important for you to grasp that real editors are not in the business of ignoring any serious problems. Editors are paid to recognize problems and recommend solutions.

Editors are people whose experience enables them to recognize and keep in mind at all times the personality and experience of a writer, the purpose of the writer's work, the style the writer employs, and the theme or themes the writer is attempting to address. And using their experience, editors go about evaluating the writer's success in accomplishing his or her goals.

Further, editors are people whose experience enables them to put themselves into the place of the target reader when reading the writer's work.

> Editors are in the best position to evaluate a writer's work because in addition to understanding so many issues the writer is dealing with in writing for the readers, the editor is in fact one of the earliest readers of the manuscript—if not the very first reader.

You might have noticed that each of the previous three paragraphs began with the words, "Editors are people." Here are four additional thoughts on that.

1. Editors are indeed people, which means they, like the authors they edit, are fallible creatures.

2. Since editors are fallible, authors should give them some slack and not expect perfection from them—especially after only the first pass through a manuscript. Depending on the complexity of the manuscript, a book may need to be edited several times before it's ready to be submitted to a potential publisher for review.

3. Since both author *and* editor are fallible, just as authors can let their pride get in the way of patiently considering the advice and guidance of an editor, an editor can also allow pride to get in the way of fostering a good relationship with the author he or she is editing.

4. No author should have to deal with editors who view themselves as the world's supreme authorities on writing—or to put it bluntly, grammar gods or protectors and gate keepers of the English language.

While most editors I've met have been great to work with, some are not. And that's too bad. All editors should be compassionate and encourage writers as much as possible. Editors should be willing and apt to teach and show their students understanding, compassion, and humility.

But that said, writers should *not* go into editing expecting professional editors to constantly provide to them only positive comments or an "attaboy" or "attagirl." That's not their job.

Using Friends and Family Members as Editors

Using friends and family members as *editors* isn't usually a good idea (depending on the results you expect). And there are reasons for that.

1. Friends and family members may not have any more experience in writing than you do.

2. Even if a friend or family member has experience in editing, you should consider if you can really trust him or her to be frank with you when it comes to dealing with any serious issues that may appear in your manuscript.

It's been said that a true friend can tell you anything. I assume that's possible when you have an enduring and close friendship bound with the strongest of tough-love chords. But it's best to understand that friends generally want to stay friends. And as for family members, they can often keep opinions to themselves because they don't want to cause trouble.

In order for a writer to produce the best manuscript possible, the writer needs the critical eye of an editor who isn't only well equipped to do the work but also willing to put excellence in written communication above any friendship that may develop between the author and the editor.

A qualified editor shouldn't be bound by any attachment to the author that limits the editor's ability to be up-front and honest. It's wonderful for authors and editors to form friendships, but that must *not* be the highest priority in author/editor relations.

Peer Reviews in Lieu of the Use of a Qualified Editor

Although peer reviews can be meaningful and helpful to a writer when properly handled, they don't take the place of thorough editing by a qualified editor. By all means, send a chapter, or even a complete draft, to a peer for preliminary feedback on your work if you like, but don't depend only on that to help you make your manuscript the absolute best it can be.[3]

---

3   Note: The term "Peer Review" here doesn't refer to academic peer reviews. It refers to submission to ministerial or professional peers relative to any position or profession of the writer.

— Chapter 8 —

Getting the Most Out of Editing

LET'S BE HONEST and open about this; "Being edited is the pits." I'm actually quoting myself here, because this is something I commonly tell authors who come to me for editing.

I like to be up-front with authors and let them know I understand what they're likely to go through. And I understand it because I've been on both sides of the table. Long before I edited someone else's work, I was edited. And while my first editor was a joy to work with, the next one I worked with was not.

My first editor was also my literary agent, David A. Womack. He's gone now and resides with the Lord. But I'll never forget all the things he taught me. David was an Assemblies of God pastor, evangelist, overseas missionary, and highly respected author of several books. When I met him, he was the Manager of Book Publishing at Gospel Publishing House in Springfield, Missouri.

When he left his position with Gospel Publishing House he began focusing on evangelistic work, but he also decided to open a literary agency to help people like me get published. As my editor he helped me polish my manuscript. Then as my agent he successfully placed my book with a publisher.

I was pleased with the book and was excited to go to work with the publisher's copyeditor to get the book into its final condition for printing. But my excitement soon ended when I began to be challenged by the copyeditor.

In the whole process, it wasn't really a lot of changes that had to be made to the manuscript that caused me anguish; it was the fact that so much of my work was being questioned. But even that wouldn't have been all that much of a problem if I hadn't had to spend time explaining my work to a copyeditor who seemed to always approach me as if he'd been eating sour grapes.

He seemed to have little compassion for me as a new author, and I felt like sometimes he treated me with contempt. From the moment he started work on my manuscript to the time he was done, I felt like I was dying a thousand deaths at the hand of an annoyed expert I wished I hadn't been forced to have as a partner.[4]

Because of that experience, when I started editing the work of others I determined to do everything I could to help authors understand the process ahead of time. I wanted them to be at least somewhat prepared mentally and emotionally for dealing with an editor—even a grouchy one, which I try not to be.

---

4   Although that was a challenging and sometimes miserable experience for me, it hasn't been repeated to that degree. And in time I came to have respect for even that tough, grouchy editor, because I learned some valuable things from him that helped me improve as a writer. And who knows what kind of an editor I would be today without having had that experience? Love people, hold no animosities, and count all experiences as opportunities to learn.

But beyond that, I also determined to do what I could to never allow myself to become seen by anyone as a domineering overlord of the English language.

Managing Expectations

I hope you'll have an editor who'll encourage you in every way he or she can. However, you need to expect any editor worth his or her fees to point out problems in your work, not ignore them.

Dealing with Emotions

Sometimes a problem an editor finds in your work may be significant and cause you grief, attack your pride, and perhaps even anger you. If at a minimum you'll entertain the idea that such a thing could happen, at least you won't be completely surprised if it does.

If that happens to you, take your time dealing with your emotions before responding to the editor about how you feel about what the editor did in the way of making changes to your manuscript (from minor modifications to deletions). The editor will be willing to discuss it.

> If you have a good editor, the editor's goal is to make your work stronger, not merely make your work conform to rules of grammar.

Making your work stronger should be one of your own primary goals from the beginning to the end of your manuscript's development. And keeping that in mind will help you deal with personal disappointments during the editing process.

Maintaining High Standards

After having your manuscript edited by a competent editor, you'll then move on to publishing your book. Unless you self-publish with an individual or company that doesn't have or enforce high standards—and especially if you have the privilege of being published by a traditional publisher— you'll not only have to deal with the publisher's copyeditor but also meet the standards maintained by that publisher.

If you have your book accepted by a traditional publisher, don't expect to have your way in every stage of either copyediting or publishing. But if you were wise and paid a professional editor to work with you on your manuscript prior to submitting it, you'll see the benefits of that decision. You'll look back and be thankful for the editing process even if going through it was painful at the time.

Assuming your editor has experience working with publishers, the editor will have a good feel for what shape your manuscript should be in to be accepted by a publisher. And if the editor has done a good job partnering with you on your manuscript, your experience with the publisher's copyeditor will be much better than it could have been had you submitted your manuscript prior to thorough editing.

> Your book will be stronger after the pain of being edited, and you'll be better prepared for your next writing project.

Process

Regardless of whether you partner with an editor to help you develop a manuscript chapter by chapter or supply an editor with a completed manuscript, the procedure of editing will be pretty much the same. You'll supply your work to the editor; the editor will read your work, mark it up or edit it as necessary, write comments, and return it to you. I can't speak for all editors, but I'll read and edit the work at least two times, and sometimes even more, before returning it.

The author is then tasked with reviewing the changes, reading the editor's notes, and responding to them. The author shouldn't dismiss lightly any of the editor's work. Take it seriously, and don't allow *pure emotion alone* to lead you into making decisions to challenge the editor's efforts. You as the author, however, do have every right to question the editor's work, ask for clarifications, and make requests. But understand that the editor also has not only the right but the responsibility to respond.

At the end of the process, which I like to view as a partnership, you and your editor will hopefully have come to an agreement on edits, but that's not always the case. Sometimes you just have to agree to disagree and move on.

The process I personally follow to actually do the initial editing itself is to use Microsoft Word to edit a manuscript electronically with all lines single spaced, like they will be when reading the book. I no longer want to deal with double spaced lines since I no longer use an editor's traditional markup language and red ink to mark up a paper copy.

It's much more efficient for me these days to simply use Microsoft Word's *Track Changes* functionality to actually make the corrections I want the writer to make instead of taking time to tell the writer to do something and have the writer do it. This partially explains how I view the author *partnering* with an editor. I also use the "New Comment" function in Word to place comments in the right-hand margin of the page.

When it comes to adding comments, I may spend more time doing that than many editors. I often spend time explaining some of the edits when I feel I should. And in some of those explanations I go to considerable lengths in my attempt to help the writer understand the reasons for the edits. This comes from my tendency to not only fix problems but also teach.

But there's even more to be gained from editing electronically using *Track Changes*. When sending files to the writer to review my edits, I generate a PDF document to send to the author. It's printed from the work file that shows all the changes I made and all the comments I added. Then after copying the work file to one with its name ending in "All Edits Accepted," I use the Track Changes reviewing functionality to accept all the changes in the copied file. I then also delete all the comments and save the copied file.

After all the changes are accepted and the comments are deleted from the copied and renamed file, I then have a file to send to the author that shows the author exactly what the work looks like after editing if all my edits are accepted. Assuming the vast majority of edits will not be questioned, the author can simply use the "All Edits Accepted" file to make any additional changes if that's how the author would like to handle it.

When it comes to processes, I prefer them to be efficient. And up to now this has worked out pretty well for both me and the authors I've edited.

Responsibilities

Getting your manuscript into the best shape it can be in should be seen as a shared responsibility. And I stress to many authors I edit that the shared responsibility of editing will not be finished until the typeset copy of the book is accepted and goes to press. (I follow the book through every stage of publishing if that's part of my agreement with the author.)

I make sure the author knows there's plenty of time to discuss changes to the manuscript, and no edits or changes that the author or I make are set in stone until the printer receives the typeset manuscript. (Of course, only very minor changes should be made during the typesetting phase.)

Responsibilities of the Editor

Before editing begins, authors and editors should discuss and come to agreement on the type or depth of editing needed for the manuscript. From my standpoint as an editor, I want to have some comfort level in the author's willingness to go through the editing process—especially if I see a lot of problems I'm going to need to address. And I feel a responsibility to be open with the author as to how I go about my work.

Here are some points I share with authors about how I view my own responsibilities as an editor. Keep in mind that all editors may not feel the same way, and I suggest you make sure you agree up front with any editor you have as a partner concerning how he or she feels about these responsibilities.

1. Protecting the Interests of the Author

   As an editor, I feel a high responsibility to protect the interests of the author and make sure I do all I can to strengthen the author's work while maintaining the author's voice and style. (And more on my feelings about protecting the interests of the author is contained in point three, below.)

2. Protecting the Interests of the Publisher

As an editor I also feel a responsibility to protect the interests of publishers. Having worked with a publisher one-on-one, I understand a publisher's needs and expectations. I also have what I think is a decent reputation to maintain—not only with authors but also publishers.

3. Upholding Biblical Standards

Just as Christian publishers have standards for the books they publish—standards that go beyond styles and formatting—I also have standards and feelings of responsibility to show myself worthy of God's trust in handling basic Christian doctrines and Scriptural truth. To put this another way, I also have a responsibility to protect the interests of God and His work.

But further, my interests in Scriptural truth affect how I view my responsibility toward authors. For I don't only prioritize making an author's book as strong and as attractive as it can be to readers; I also prioritize protecting the reputation of the author. I'll examine the author's use and application of Scripture and bring to the author's attention anything that's controversial or could be construed by the reader as being in Scriptural error.

And I often tell authors that while there's no inherent problem with taking even a controversial stand as long as that stand can be reasonably backed up by Scripture, there's nothing to be gained by exposing ourselves to our readers' criticism if there's no reason for it.

In other words, there's no need to get into a fight if there's nothing to be gained by fighting.

Remember, I'm a retired minister, so it's not surprising that I have strong views on this. And there are plenty of editors who have no association with Christian ministry at all. You don't need to use the services of an editor with a background in dealing with Christian doctrine; that choice is up to you.

But if you want someone to be your sounding board, hold you accountable when dealing with Scripture, and watch your back, you should enlist an editor who can fulfill that role.

Learning

When God created us, He gave us the ability to learn. That's a gift we should never fail to use. And I really do mean *never*. The business of learning shouldn't be relegated to any particular level of formal education. And it shouldn't stop when we retire from a professional career.

I firmly believe we're meant to learn continually, and our education shouldn't end as long as we have cognitive abilities and there's breath left in our lungs. With that in mind, all writers should want to continually improve their abilities to write and communicate to their readers.

> Being edited is one of those things that provide a good opportunity to learn.

When it comes to learning, determine to take advantage of every opportunity.

Learning by Steps

As I work on this manuscript, I'm seventy years old. I've been around the block a few times, and I've learned some things (even though I often tell people I've forgotten more than I ever learned). And among the things I've learned is that God is so good—and God's wisdom, ways, and abilities are so far beyond ours—He can be trusted to lead us through every stage of our lives for His purpose.

I won't take the time to get into details, and this is somewhat of a repeat, but God has proven to me (I've learned) that every step in my life—my career development, my ministry, my discipleship, the development of my abilities, or however you would like to put it—has led me and enabled me to do what I'm doing right now.

As I've indicated already, I believe strongly in the truth of Romans 8:28.

God really does take all the things we experience in life—both the good and the bad—and uses them to bring good to us for His purpose. The only question is whether or not we take advantage of what He's doing.

My advice to writers is not to view editing as something that's a necessary evil but as an opportunity to learn new skills. Expect God to use the editor to facilitate learning. Then trust God to one day prove to you that He arranged for that learning to enable you to do what you're called upon to do on that day.

Living Through Learning

I actually went into quite a bit of detail early in the book on the subject of learning. And here I am talking about it again.

By now you must assume the topic of learning is important to me. I'll try not to be too repetitive here, but I do want to hammer home a few things that are worth repeating. And here they are:

If the Lord is calling you to write, do it. And don't feel like you can't. God doesn't call people to do things they can't do. God is more than capable of giving to you everything you'll need to perform any task He calls you to do. There's nothing wrong with stepping out to accomplish something you've never done. And as I've mentioned before, learning by doing is often the most effective way to learn.

Begin your manuscript, and God will give you what you need to complete it. And that even goes for God giving you a partner to edit your work. I believe you should view your editor as your partner. But I also believe you should find an editor who feels the same way about you.

Avoid any editor whose relationship with you is expected to be as thin as a dollar bill. Your interest in a writing project as a Christian writer needs to go beyond any financial reward you believe you'll gain by writing. And a Christian editor's interest should also be larger than any editing fee.

A worker is worthy of receiving wages. That's a biblical concept (1 Timothy 5:18). But if God is really calling you to write, and if God has appointed a helper to you in the form of an editor, the value of your project goes far beyond what the editor earns and beyond what you ever hope to receive from the project.

> In importance, if your project is from God,
> it's so significant that both you and the editor
> should put the highest priority on completing
> the project, finishing it well, and hearing
> God say, "Well done."
> That will be your greatest reward.

If you've never been edited, don't worry; you'll live through the learning. And if you go into it and through it with the right attitude and use being edited as an educational experience, what you learn will prepare you for the next step in your ministry as a Christian writer.

The Definition of Success

In this section I get into talking about the overall success of your writing project. I speak of the success of producing and publishing a book. But I'm still framing this in the context of how editing fits into that.

For the sake of dealing with the subject here, let's break down success in writing and becoming a published author into the following stages.

1. Success in finishing the manuscript
2. Success in finding a good editor
3. Success in the author and editor producing an excellent final proof
4. Success in finding a good publisher and getting the book accepted
5. Success in the book's release
6. Success in marketing, promotions, distribution, et cetera
7. Success in sales

Unless an author is a well-known personality, has a famous name, has a huge following, has connections and deep pockets to pay for hiring publicists, or already has a reputation of being a best-selling author, success defined by the volume of sales of a new book is certainly not guaranteed.

Any new author who doesn't fit into any of these categories needs to know the dream of placing a book with a big top-tier publisher and receiving an amazing advance on royalties upon signing a publishing contract is likely a dream that won't be realized regardless of the good work by you and your editor.

But my modest book here isn't directed toward best-selling authors anyway. Most of you who read this book will, like me, definitely welcome any success that comes your way. And if I'm correct, your decision to write won't hinge on any promise of notoriety. Your dream also will not likely be to land a huge book deal that will allow you to buy an island in the Caribbean.

All authors want their books to sell and reach large numbers in readership, but for Christian writers—at least I hope for you and me—we'll define *success* as having followed our callings, as having produced an excellent product that will please God, and as having our books placed into the hands of those whose lives and eternities are affected in positive ways by reading them.

Attitudes and the Part They Play

To reach *success* as I've just defined it (and I hope you agree), we'll need to choose to follow the paths laid out for us by the Holy Spirit and determine in our hearts to have attitudes that please God.

As you should have already gathered, I have strong feelings about *all* of us entering into our work with proper attitudes. As for editors' attitudes, they need to maintain good attitudes just as writers do. Editors need to go into their work realizing that writers suffer pain when work they've slaved over for sometimes years is challenged, changed, or cut from their manuscripts.

And perhaps if the more arrogant *Keepers of the Keys* of English would remember back to when they themselves suffered the pain of having their early work sliced and diced, they might have more compassion for the writers—especially the new authors.

But here's my challenge for you as a writer. Regardless of the attitude you discover in an editor whom you use to edit your book, always determine to present to the Lord an attitude on your part that the Holy Spirit can use to increase your knowledge and experience.

> We can't control the attitudes of others, but we can and hopefully will control our own.

Even if your editor seems unfeeling or unkind, assume your editor knows things you need to learn. Don't let your own attitude form a wall that keeps you from learning. Thank the editor for the help and take his or her knowledge with you when you part.

— Chapter 9 —

Writing Styles and Tones

WRITERS NEED TO be able to understand and employ the writing style and tone appropriate for the readers they're addressing. But the decision on the best style and tone for their work can also hinge on the purpose of the content. I address four writing styles below, and I've made some general comments on how they differ.

Conversational Writing

Using a conversational style in writing establishes a closer relationship between the writer and the reader. As people read the words of a writer employing a conversational style, each reader feels more like the writer is speaking personally to him or her.

A conversational style is often used in Christian writing because the writer wants to convey to the reader personal concern. While a great deal of serious issues, warnings, and admonitions can be included in the writer's words, the writer's conversational tone allows for showing greater empathy, feeling, and compassion for the reader and the reader's needs.

Following are some general guidelines on the use of conversational writing.

1. Use active voice.

    Avoid writing in passive voice. Refer to Chapter 27 for more on this. While it's best to avoid passive voice as much as possible in all writing, it's definitely more at home in formal writing styles.

2. Use contractions.

    The use of contractions (e.g., "that's" instead of "that is," and "we're" instead of "we are," etc.) becomes important when setting a conversational tone. And it's because that's the way we talk to one another—hence, conversational. (By the way, just in case you don't know, the "e.g." I used within the parentheses above means "for example.")

    The more casual we want to be in conversational writing, the more contractions we'll use. The less casual we want our writing to be, the fewer contractions we'll use.

    But be careful when proofing your work for the use of contractions if you're using your word processor's *search and replace* function. For instance, you must not use "Replace All" to replace all occurrences of "that is" to "that's." That kind of change isn't always appropriate.

    Also, be aware that it's sometimes necessary to avoid using a contraction when you want to place more emphasis on the words. For instance, the word, "is," can't be emphasized when it's part of a contraction.

3. Avoid complex wording and structure.

    Unless you're writing for children, don't write like you are. But definitely do what you can to avoid complex phrasing and sentence structure in conversational writing as much as possible. That's actually hard for some of us.

It's good to opt for using simpler, more commonly-used synonyms or terms rather than words some of your readers might not be familiar with. And sometimes it's best to rewrite sentences to keep from using difficult words and phrasing.

> When it comes to word choices, it never hurts to make use of a thesaurus. I use the thesaurus function in Microsoft Word a lot. And sometimes when I'm not satisfied with Word's thesaurus, I type words into a web browser and use its search engine to do research on words.

4. Keep sentences as short as possible.

In other words, in conversational writing, don't write like the Apostle Paul, who has long been known for writing sentences that go on for far too long. (Of course saying this has nothing at all to do with the great respect I have for Paul and the value of his words.)

Some writers have the tendency to write long, complex sentences. I admit to being one of them. In conversational writing, focus on writing short sentences. And it's absolutely appropriate in conversational writing to start sentences with conjunctions to write in shorter sentences—like I started this one.

5. Don't become too familiar with the reader.

Even within the realm of conversational writing, the writer's chosen tone can be controlled and differ from mildly casual to very casual. In conversational writing we're intentionally doing what we can to draw the reader in toward us in relationship, but we still shouldn't get too casual.

After all, everyone has some feelings about maintaining personal space. Some readers are huggers while others are hand shakers. Don't offend the hand shakers.

To illustrate, writing a sentence that begins with something like, "Honey, believe me . . ." will be seen by most readers as condescending. Don't write to me like that. I'm not your honey.

And using wording like, "Friend, I'm sure that . . . ," or, "Dear reader . . . " will also turn off a lot of readers. And especially if used more than once, it can get plumb obnoxious and be seen by some readers as repetitive and a sign of a newbie writer and unaccomplished communicator.

6. Sometimes there's a need to change tone.

   Even in conversational writing, a more professional or formal tone may be necessary at times when dealing with certain matters. That's a judgment call.

Formal Writing

Just as a conversational style of writing sets a more casual tone and brings the writer and reader into a closer relationship, a formal style does the opposite.

Note the following when producing formal writing.

1. Use Passive Voice if necessary.

   As I mentioned above, the passive voice starts becoming more acceptable in formal writing. But it's still best to avoid using passive voice as much as you can.

2. Use more of a business tone.

   One way to think of a formal style is that it sets a tone that's more proper when dealing with the *business end of things*—even if the business end of things is still the business within families like the family of God.

3. Avoid the use of contractions in formal writing.

   The lack of contractions may make the delivery of the message stiffer compared to a message written in a conversational tone, but that's indeed what it's supposed to do in formal writing.

   We want to be precise in all forms of writing, but in conversational writing we back off of sounding so, let's say, *proper*. Not so in formal writing. Of course even in formal writing, we don't want to come across to the reader as overly stiff in our delivery, but we do in fact want to be seen as more proper in our speech.

4. The use of a more formal style and tone puts more space between the author (perhaps teacher?) and the reader (student?).

   This doesn't mean we can't have a friendly, meaningful relationship with our reader, it just means we're less personal in our approach and more professional in addressing our reader.

Technical Writing

Prior to my entry into other forms of writing, I gained experience in technical writing. That's actually where I cut my teeth, so to speak, in writing. While working several years as a Civil Engineering Technician for the City of Stillwater, Oklahoma, I wrote bid documents, contracts, and work specifications.

While there, I also designed and produced plans for the construction of various public works projects, like water and sewer systems and street construction. All that work—both plans and the previously mentioned documents associated with them—had to be produced in an exact manner. And serious problems could arise if they were not, including legal and public health issues.

I view technical writing as formal writing on steroids. Those involved in technical writing—especially when dealing with legal issues—deal with a great quantity of what I call *minutia*. The misuse of a single word's meaning or comma can get you into serious trouble. Your company can get sued. You can be fired for not making sure "every '*t*' has been crossed and every '*i*' has been dotted."

Being involved in that work was a good learning experience, and it helped lay the foundation for what I'm doing today. Most of you who are reading this likely won't have the same experience in your careers. But that's not a problem. That's just how I learned some things; that doesn't mean you need to learn like that.

And by the way, I'm not using anything close to the same style of writing in this book. You should be glad. I could be that formal, but what would that gain either you or me? You see, with experience, you too can *choose* how to write.

> You can write with different styles and tone depending on what's best for your purpose. Just make sure you always keep that purpose and your readership firmly in mind as you write.

Academic Writing

I cover things in this book that will hopefully be helpful to someone involved in academic writing. But this book definitely isn't focused on that style of writing, so I won't get into much directly related to it.

It's possible writers who read this may need to apply such a style sometime in their work. There could be a need to write a thesis for a theology class. Or there may even be an interest in participating in writing content for doctrinal commentary. So I'll make a few comments.

In academic writing, an author will employ a formal style and professional tone to his or her work—such as is expected or required for presentation to readers with an academic interest. And while academic writing may not require an author to speak or write *legalese* like those involved in many forms of technical writing, the author of an academic work still needs to stay attentive to writing with great precision and expected formality.

And of course if the academic interest involves theology, the writer may use words like exegesis, hermeneutics, Parousia, transubstantiation, beatific vision, Christological, Deuteronomistic, ecclesiology, eschatology, . . . In my opinion, if your readership is not made up of theologians, you should find other ways to express yourself.

My main advice for anyone involved in academic writing is to make sure you avail yourself of the guidance provided for that kind of writing contained in a reputable style guide like *The Chicago Manual of Style*. And if you're writing for a specific class in school, you should discuss with the professor about the style guide he or she prefers.

One thing for sure, if a person has experience with academic writing and is prone to automatically use an academic style, that person should consciously determine *not* to do that when writing for a broader readership.

> Don't write with an academic style if your focused readership is a general audience. And definitely don't do that if you want your writing to reach or connect with non-believers who live outside of academic circles.

Consistency

Regardless of the style you use in your writing, there's always a need for consistency throughout every manuscript. And this is something the editor will be focused on like a laser.

If you're writing in a casual, conversational style in order to establish a closer relationship with your reader, be consistent in maintaining that style throughout the manuscript.

If you're developing a work using a conversational style—and many who read this will—review the list of guidelines I placed above under the section, "Conversational Writing." If you do your best to follow them in your writing before you place your manuscript in the hands of an editor, you'll have less red ink to contend with.

— Chapter 10 —

Style Guides

STYLE GUIDES CONSIST of an accumulation of published guidelines followed by writers when producing their work. Style guides are based on accepted rules of grammar but also deal with various preferences that go beyond simple rules.

Some guidelines, or rules, will be agreed upon and placed in every respected style guide, while other guidelines on how to handle things may differ from one style guide to another. There's not one style guide that all disciplines or educators agree to use. Even individual departments within the same university may adopt and follow different style guides.

Following, below, are three style guides writers need to be familiar with or at least know about.

The Chicago Manual of Style

Among style guides approved by book publishers in America, *The Chicago Manual of Style* is the most popular. It's very comprehensive in nature, and it's been updated several times since it was first published. Each update recognizes and reflects changes in the English language and acceptable styles of writing that happen over time.

As of the date of this writing, the current version of the *Chicago Manual* is "CMOS 17." (My copy is CMOS 15.) Hard copies of the *Chicago Manual* are a trusted possession in the libraries of a large number of writers. But today a writer may also subscribe to an online version.

When subscribed to the online version, a writer can also take advantage of a discussion list used by people to ask questions of the authorities at the University of Chicago, where the *Chicago Manual* has been produced by the University of Chicago Press since 1906.

Visit https://www.chicagomanualofstyle.org to get more information about *The Chicago Manual of Style*.

The AP Stylebook

The Associated Press Stylebook is a writing style guide developed by American journalists connected with the Associated Press journalism cooperative based in New York City. And as someone writing on *Wikipedia* describes it, "although it is sold as a guide for reporters, it has become the leading reference for most forms of public-facing corporate communication over the last half-century."[5]

In other words, the acceptance of recommendations from *The AP Stylebook* on English grammar, capitalization, abbreviations, punctuation, spelling, and citations has spilled over from its use by news and media outlets to become broadly applied in many sectors. However, it's still not the primary style guide chosen by most book publishers.

According to the web site, https://www.apstylebook. com/, *The AP Stylebook* is in its 56th edition since it was first published in 1953.

---

5   https://en.wikipedia.org/wiki/AP_Stylebook, accessed February 9, 2023.

The Publisher's Style Guide

There are other style guides in addition to the two most prevalent ones—*Chicago* and *AP*. Most are style guides dedicated for use in various individual disciplines. But it's more important for you to know that publishers also develop their own style guides used for editing and publishing their books.

For instance, publishers will adopt *The Chicago Manual of Style* for their companies and apply the majority of its guidelines but then tweak it a bit here and there to reflect how they want writers to handle various aspects of their writing.

For authors whose books are accepted for publishing, writers need to prioritize following the Publisher's Style Guide over either *Chicago* or *AP*. But if you don't have a publisher, start by following the *Chicago Manual*.

—Chapter 11—

Chapters and Themes

BEFORE STARTING WORK on a manuscript, a writer will have a theme in mind for the work. (Of course after working on the manuscript, the writer may decide to take a different approach or even decide to change the theme.) No book is an organized work if it doesn't have a strong and clear central theme that the entirety of the book revolves around.

In addition to a strong theme, every book should have an attractive title that reflects the book's theme. After that's established, the overall message of the book will be divided up into reasonable divisions, or chapters. And each of those should have an attractive title that reflects the respective, individual division's or chapter's theme—which in effect will be a subtheme used to address and complete the author's handling of the book's central theme.

Supporting the Book's Theme

When developing your manuscript, make sure both the content and title of each chapter firmly fit logically within and complement or enhance the book's theme.

> If either a title or the content of a chapter doesn't directly support or add real value to addressing the book's central theme, don't use it.

If there isn't a direct and apparent link between a chapter and the book's theme—which also assumes there won't be a direct link between a chapter and the other chapters—that chapter needs to be either removed or rewritten to bring it into a tight relationship with the book's theme.

Limiting Content to the Chapter's Theme

As for the content of chapters supporting the chapters' main points, or subthemes within the book's overarching theme, it's important for writers not to allow themselves to get distracted or pulled off point when developing each chapter's content. Make sure all the content within each chapter fits firmly within and complements or relates to that chapter's main point.

Sometimes we can find ourselves guilty of interjecting stray thoughts into our work that make sense to us at the time but lead readers' minds off on tangents. It's sometimes all too easy to have a thought suddenly pop into our minds and then start following that thought when we shouldn't deal with it at that moment. Those are thoughts that lead away from dealing with the chapter's main point.

We need to be careful not to interject into a chapter, or into any paragraph within a chapter, any content that doesn't fit within the flow of thought we've established. We need to be careful not to switch gears by inserting anything into our work that will take the readers' minds off on a journey away from the chapter's theme—especially if we don't have an effective way to bring them back.

There's more on the *flow of thought* in the next chapter.

It's crucial that we catch and correct interjections that interfere with our attempts to keep the minds of the readers moving toward a relevant and effective ending to each chapter. While proofing your work, always make a point to evaluate your work *critically* to see if everything you've written has a connection to the chapter's theme. If it doesn't, change it or get rid of it.

Ending on Point

It's been said that the two most important things about a performance—like a play or a musical or vocal presentation—is how one starts and how one ends. I think there's a certain truth in that and how it carries over to writing.

How a writer starts is like leaving a first impression. First impressions are important. And as we continue writing, everything we write works toward giving readers expectations. Hopefully every chapter ends well and leads to another chapter that also ends well. But even if there are glitches here and there—if not every chapter is so strong—the writer still anticipates a strong closing to the book.

When we close a chapter, we need to be careful to end the chapter with a statement that brings a logical end to addressing that chapter's main point. And without needing to mention or repeat all the main points we made in each chapter in the book, we also need to finish the book with an appealing and effective ending that wraps up our handling of the book's overall theme.

> Your reader will always anticipate a strong and compelling ending. A good ending pulls it all together. And the way we end is critically important since we need to satisfy the reader's expectations.

When a person is listening to a live performance, while that person may notice problems during the performance, as long as the performance both begins well and ends well, there's at least a chance the listener will forgive the performer for problems in between. The listener knows the performer is human, and humans make mistakes.

There's the old adage that says, "All's well that ends well." Perhaps that saying (right or wrong) is a good thing for us to keep in mind as we write; because the beginning and ending of our writing are indeed extremely important. And especially when it comes to the ending, that's what we leave with our reader as our parting gesture. There's no making up for it if we blow the ending.

When you get to the final chapter of your book, you'll have either met readers' expectations or disappointed them. You either answered their questions or left them with more questions. You either left them thinking you're a good writer or left them thinking you need to improve.

Always end on point.

Make sure your closing statements are related to and bring a meaningful conclusion to the theme you established when you started the chapter. And write in a way that in every chapter you tie the chapter's theme back to the book's theme.

Start on point. Stay on point. And end on point.

Chapter 12

Flow of Thought

WE HAVE RESPONSIBILITIES as writers. We have a responsibility to write with clarity. We have a responsibility to write with a style that will help us connect with our audience. We have a responsibility to develop compelling, logical, and enriching thoughts to feed the readers' minds. But we need to go beyond that.

We also have a huge responsibility to organize all our wonderful thoughts into a comfortable-flowing message that's easy to follow and holds the interest of readers.

Seasoned and accomplished writers don't simply gather together a lot of great thoughts, plonk them down in a haphazard way, and let the readers sort them out. If we want to be successful communicators in writing, we must recognize and fulfill our responsibility to establish, organize, and maintain a unified, comfortable flow of thought throughout our work.

Leading the Mind

A good writer doesn't just write. A good writer knowingly and purposely captures and controls the focus of the reader and then leads the reader's mind through the material the writer develops. I don't know how to say it in a clearer way.

Either you understand, remember, and fulfill this critical responsibility or you don't. Your success as a writer may actually hinge on your ability to keep your reader's mind focused and on track. And your reputation in the eyes of the reader will at least to some degree always be linked to how easy you make it for the reader to follow your line of reasoning and logic.

To be a success in the reader's eyes, you must definitely prioritize and succeed in doing two things. First, you must write in a way that allows the reader to understand what you're saying. Second, your words and methods must not only appeal to and feed the reader's mind, they must actually capture and lead your reader's mind to where it needs to go step by step throughout the book.

I'm intentionally repeating "capture." To lead the reader's mind you must indeed first *capture* it. You'll capture it when you successfully entice it and draw it into your story or narrative. Then after it's captured, you hold it and guide it through your work by keeping it focused and moving through your story or narrative in a smooth, logical manner. Doing that is one of your most important challenges.

> Your challenge is to establish a compelling flow of thought and keep that flow of thought moving in a smooth, logical way until you lead the reader's mind all the way to your closing statement.

Maintaining the flow of thought is tantamount to *continually* feeding and leading the reader's mind. When writing sentences, the thought in each sentence must somehow flow from, relate to, or build on what was written in the previous sentence. And the thought contained in that sentence must somehow flow into the next one in a way to set up the mind of the reader to accept what is said in that sentence.

The same must happen between paragraphs. A cohesive and logical thought must flow unimpeded and smoothly from one sentence to another and from one paragraph to another. If it doesn't, the reader will not be able to stick with you throughout your work.

Strategic Breaks

Maintaining a proper flow of thought from one sentence to another throughout each paragraph and chapter—basically throughout the entire book—is critical. But that doesn't mean there can't be breaks in the flow of thought here and there. It simply means that any breaks in the flow of thought must be *managed*.

Inadvertent breaks or interruptions in the flow of thought *must* be avoided. But intentional, well-managed, planned breaks (as long as they're appropriate and lead to a strategic result) are often useful and even necessary.

To wrap your mind around the concept of *intentional* and *planned* breaks, think of the largest breaks in a book— the ones between chapters. Those breaks are absolutely intentional and planned. With breaks between chapters, one major point relevant to the theme of the book is finished, and another major point begins.

Just as you have multiple chapters in a book, you can have multiple sections and even subsections in a chapter. And just as we signal to the reader that the flow of thought is being broken with chapter breaks, we do the same with section and subsection breaks. They're intended breaks, and they're properly managed. They serve a purpose, and they make sense.

If properly organized and developed, the major point in each chapter in a book leads methodically toward completing the writer's work of dealing with the book's overarching theme. Likewise, properly developed sections and subsections within chapters lead toward the successful completion of the individual chapter's point.

> Chapters are basically individual, major points made while developing the *book's* overall theme for the reader. And sections and subsections within a chapter contain separate, organized thoughts used to develop the *chapter's* point.

Section and Subsection Breaks

There are two section breaks in this chapter above this location. And each section has a title. They are, "**Leading the Mind**," and, "**Strategic Breaks**."

NOTE: Depending on the style used in a book, its organization, and its content, you will often see chapters with section breaks that don't have titles. Such breaks without titles are commonly introduced to the reader with some kind of section break graphic, or divider line, to signal the break.

Then directly above, you'll see the title signaling the break in the flow of thought for this subsection: "Section and Subsection Breaks," which is organized within the section titled **Strategic Breaks**.

Whether we're dealing with section breaks or subsection breaks, with their use we're signaling to the reader that we're shifting gears in the flow of thought. We're intentionally either going in a different direction for a while or we're simply breaking up our point into pieces. And for either reason, we'll make sure the reader understands why we did it as we complete our thoughts.

> **IMPORTANT:** Anytime we insert a *managed* break to inject a thought or idea that leads the reader's mind in a different direction, after we finish that thought it's extremely important that we somehow methodically reconnect the reader's mind back into the main flow of thought.

Other Strategic Breaks

If we're to be successful in shepherding the reader's mind through our material and keeping it engaged and on point, we must always let the reader know what we're thinking and where we're going.

Even shorter breaks in the flow of thought (very short interjections) are manageable and sometimes useful if handled properly. But regardless, the reader needs a signal that the writer knows what he or she is doing. The reader needs to *know* the break in thought wasn't an accident. The writer needs to somehow show the reader how the interjection relates to the already-established flow of thought.

Depending on what's needed to hold the reader's attention and keep the reader's mind from drifting off point when adding such an interjection, the signal we give to the reader can be merely a simple statement, or it may require a more thorough explanation.

Signals we give the reader can be somewhat creative or pretty common statements—depending on what's required. And they can come before the break in thought or after—whatever works considering the context.

An appropriate signal could consist of, "I know this isn't completely relevant, but . . . " Or a signal after the fact could be something like, "Just hold that thought while we get back on point."

All that said, it's best if you avoid short interjections in the flow of thought. But the worst interruption is one that was neither *intentional* nor *managed*.

Avoiding Tangents

As you can see in the above explanations, there's a time and place for inserting breaks into the flow of thought, but to be intentionally repetitive here, I can't stress enough that any such breaks must be *deliberate* and have purpose.

> Unintended, unplanned, non-strategic breaks in the flow of thought lead readers' minds off on a tangent—away from the intended flow of thought—without leading the mind back in a deliberate, effective manner.

Did you notice how many statements in this chapter addressing **Flow of Thought** are boxed to give them special emphasis?

There are FOUR of them.

I suppose by that you might get the idea I can get pretty worked up about this. Well, you're right! But that's only because I've so often dealt with problems with writers leading their readers' minds off on tangents and, basically, *leaving them out there to dry.*

By the way, I love and respect all those writers. We built good relationships based on mutual respect and Christian love. They just needed someone to help them learn. There's no shame in that. And now they're better writers.

Please read all of this chapter again—especially this section—and get it fixed in your mind.

I stress this because it's so common for writers to inadvertently and unwittingly interrupt their flow of thought and lead their readers' minds off on a tangent. All writers don't suffer from this tendency, but all too many do. And when they interject what essentially becomes stray thoughts into their work, they confuse the reader and damage the effectiveness of their writing.

The worst examples of this are statements so abrupt that they violently *jerk* the reader's mind off point. If readers' minds are jerked back and forth enough times, the readers will definitely question the ability of the writer. And when that starts happening, the chances increase that they'll close the book in frustration.

That's never a good thing.

— Chapter 13 —

Paragraphs
and Formatting

WHEN I ACCEPT a manuscript for editing I often receive one with long paragraphs—sometimes *way too long.* But even when authors do a good job of writing in shorter paragraphs, it's inevitable that I'll still shorten some of them even more for various reasons.

I address paragraph lengths and the reasons for using shorter paragraphs below. And following that, I'll deal with paragraph styles and formatting.

Paragraph Length

Writers need to be aware of the space that paragraphs will take up in final typeset and printed books when compared to the amount of space they take up on a letter-size page in a manuscript generated in their word processing software.

Depending on the publisher's standards for book size, font size, and paragraph formatting, a very long paragraph in a letter-size document (single spaced) could possibly fill an entire page of a book half that size. A rule of thumb from many publishers is to expect an average of somewhere around 250 words per page in a printed book.

That's one reason for maintaining a focus on paragraph length. But here are some additional reasons to use shorter paragraphs—and in some cases even a one-line paragraph.

1. Shorter paragraphs make the writer's thoughts easier to read and consume in bite-sized morsels.

   Some people say a paragraph should be a minimum of three sentences long. My take is that while I often count to see how many sentences are in a paragraph, and while I may have "three" as a number in mind, I consider as a more important determining factor both the length of the sentences and the value of the statements.

   If a single sentence is somewhat long, but its structure is still plainly readable; if there's something to be gained by not breaking it up into multiple sentences; or even if short, the statement made in the sentence is in itself a strong one, I'll often set it apart as its own paragraph.

   I just did that.

2. Shorter paragraphs are used to keep valuable points or statements from being lost among or covered up by a multitude of words and other less-important sentences.

   While valuable points and statements might not seem to the writers to be covered up in long paragraphs, that's likely because the writers are *not* the ones reading the words for the first time. Writers already know and anticipate the points and statements. Readers, though, don't have that luxury.

   I suggest you read the previous paragraph again and drive a stake down by it.

   > Write for the **reader**, and that applies
   > even to paragraph lengths.

3. Sometimes very short paragraphs are used by authors when writing dialogue.

   When writing dialogue between people, the words of each speaker should be in individual paragraphs as they speak to each other in turn. And especially in dialogue, an individual paragraph will many times consist of only one sentence—even one or two words—spoken by the person taking part in the dialogue.

   > Example:
   >
   > "Where'd he go?" he enquired.
   >
   > "Home."
   >
   > "Oh," he responded, knowing that he actually couldn't have gone home.

4. Paragraphs are sometimes shortened to add additional emphasis or interest to statements or thoughts.

   I'll sometimes take a good closing sentence in a writer's paragraph and drop it down into its own paragraph even when it's a short statement. That emphasizes the statement that I broke off into its own paragraph while at the same time also placing more emphasis on the previous statement that led into it.

Paragraph Formatting

Both paragraph lengths and styles need to be consciously managed to improve the readability, focus, and clarity of the writer's message. Proper formatting of paragraphs also helps the reader follow the writer's thoughts. Good formatting will help the reader recognize not only the various types of material in the book but also how thoughts are organized.

Paragraph Styles

When developing a manuscript, I believe it's worth the writer's time to make an effort to learn how to use, apply, and modify paragraph styles that can be embedded in the manuscript. Microsoft Word, Apache OpenOffice, Apple Pages, WordPerfect, and other word processing applications support the use and modification of paragraph styles. It's a common function.

Properly configured paragraph styles saved in the manuscript file are useful in quickly formatting paragraphs. For instance, most of the paragraphs in a Microsoft Word document should have the "Normal" style applied to them by default.

If a writer learns how to modify the paragraph styles, the writer can simply modify the "Normal" style and other styles used in the document to easily switch the entire document back and forth from double spaced lines—for printing double-spaced proofs—to single spaced lines for more comfortable reading and editing on the computer.

Besides the "Normal" paragraph style, following is a list of paragraph styles that I find particularly important and useful.

1. Initial Paragraphs in Chapters, Sections, and Subsections

   With the styles I most often use, all paragraphs are completely justified both left and right. And for each initial, first paragraph that appears in chapters, sections, and subsections (the first paragraph following the break), the paragraph has no further indention on the first line of the paragraph.

So using the "Normal" style in Word as the parent style (*Style based on*), I configured and saved another *system* paragraph style in Word for initial paragraphs and named the style "Normal Initial." When I then write that first paragraph, I simply apply the *Normal Initial* style to it, and Word automatically and quickly formats the paragraph without an indention of the first line.

2. Block Quotations

Block quotations are those not written "in line" within other statements contained in the narrative. They're quotations written in separate paragraphs that are further indented both left and right compared to paragraphs formatted with the "Normal" style. And the first line of block quotation paragraphs is not further indented.

Block quotations may include more than one paragraph when dealing with long quotations. The paragraph style I configured and saved for block quotations is named "Indent."

3. Scripture Block Quotations

My recommendation is to italicize all quotations of Scripture. I address that further in the following chapter as well as in Chapter 25. The applied italics is the main difference between block quotations of passages of Scripture and other block quotations (not italicized). The paragraph style I configured for Scripture block quotations is named "Indent Italic," and this paragraph style has the default paragraph font configured as *italic*.

> Once the "Indent Italic" style is applied to a Scripture block quotation, I remove the italics from the Scripture *reference*. An example of one Scripture block quotation is below, and more on formatting quotations is in the next chapter.

Quotation Marks in Block Quotations

Quotation marks are used to begin and end quotations written in line with the rest of the narrative. But quotation marks are **not** used to begin or end block quotations. The quotation marks are omitted from block quotations unless the quotation actually begins or ends in dialogue with the speaker addressed with a dialogue tag, for instance:

> *"I will give you the glory of these kingdoms and authority over them," the devil said, "because they are mine to give anyone I please. I will give it all to you if you will worship me."*   (Luke 4:6–7)

In the above block quotation, if the tag, "the devil said," were not in the quotation, there would be no quotation marks in the block quotation at all—including the quotation marks beginning and ending the block quotation. Again, see more on formatting quotations in the next chapter.

Other Paragraph Styles

Other paragraph styles I employ in my writing and editing include those for chapter titles, section titles, and subsection titles. I suggest all writers employ paragraph styles to help them organize their material and better visualize how their book's content will be seen by the reader.

— Chapter 14 —

Quotations and References

THERE ARE ONLY a few procedures a writer needs to master when dealing with quotations and references—at least in the scope of this book. But that's no reflection on the importance of the topic.

Scripture Quotations

As already mentioned in the previous chapter, and for reasons further explained in Chapter 25, I recommend that you italicize all quoted Scriptures, including in-line quotations.

The proper form to follow for punctuating **in-line** Scripture quotations is: *"For this is how God loved the world: He gave his one and only Son, so that everyone who believes in him will not perish but have eternal life"* (John 3:16).

> Note above that when quoting Scriptures *in-line*, the period isn't placed at the end of the quoted passage. It's placed after the closing parenthesis at the end of the Scripture reference—the end of the entire sentence containing the quotation *and* reference. And the Scripture reference isn't italicized.

If the Scripture quotation itself ended with either a question mark or an exclamation point, that punctuation mark is placed at the end of the quoted passage just like it appears in Scripture, like so: *"Then the LORD said to Moses, 'Has my arm lost its power? Now you will see whether or not my word comes true!'"* (Numbers 11:23). The period is still placed at the end of the closing parenthesis to end the sentence containing the quotation.

Scriptures quoted in block quotations are placed in indented paragraphs just like other block quotations, and the quotation marks are dropped unless the quotation contains dialogue with a speaker identified with a tag (as mentioned in the previous chapter).

> *Hear, O Israel: The LORD our God, the LORD is one! You shall love the LORD your God with all your heart, with all your soul, and with all your strength. And these words which I command you today shall be in your heart.*
>
> (Deuteronomy 6:4–6 NKJV)

Note above that in a block quotation of Scripture the period stays at the end of the quoted verse; the Scripture reference isn't italicized; and there's *no* period after the reference.

Also note above that each occurrence of "ord" in the word, "LORD," is spelled with small caps. That's because if you check the spelling of "Lord" in the Old Testament and compare it to "Lord" in the New Testament, you'll find the Old Testament uses small caps, and the New Testament doesn't. Don't ask me why; that's above my pay grade.

I always make sure I proof typeset copies before going to printing. And one of the things I look for is the use of *Small caps* in "Lord" for Old Testament quotations—quotations that I already had properly formatted in the manuscript file I delivered to the publisher. It's a common thing to find the small caps getting dropped when the typesetter imports my file into the typesetting software.

With the original manuscript being edited in Microsoft Word, it's a simple thing to use "Small caps" when needed. Simply select and highlight the characters you want in small caps, choose "Font" in the right-click Context Menu, and mark the "Small caps" box.

Other Quotations

Other quotations used in the manuscript (meaning non-Scripture quotations)—both in-line quotations *and* block quotations—will be treated the same way as Scripture quotations except that non-Scripture quotations *won't be italicized*. And either footnotes or endnotes should be used for referencing non-Scripture quotations unless the reference is short enough to comfortably fit at the end of the quotation and not be visually intrusive.

Here's a simple example of a Footnote or Endnote reference number placed at the end of a quotation:

The piano teacher pointed his finger at the sheet of music in front of his student and said to her, "Every good boy does fine."[6]

---

6   The first letter of each word corresponds to the notes on the five lines of the treble staff in a music score—E G B D F.

Footnotes

When I think the reader will be interested in reading a note of explanation or be prone to care enough to look at a reference for a quotation, my preference is to always place the comment or annotation in a *footnote* for the reader's convenience at the bottom of the same page containing the footnote reference number.

Having footnotes at the bottom of the same page as the material being referenced keeps the reader from having to be more distracted than necessary by having to turn to the end of a chapter or the back of the book. In other words, it helps the reader stay engaged with the flow of thought.

Even when dealing with references, prioritize the needs of the reader.

Besides their use in referencing quotations, footnotes may also be used for providing helpful comments by the author without interrupting the flow of thought more than necessary. Or if the author wants to give the reader additional Scripture references other than one for the passage specifically quoted in either an in-line or block quotation, those references also can be added to a footnote.

> NOTE: If I put a Scripture quotation in a footnote, it's punctuated with quotation marks just like an in-line quote, but <u>I do *not* italicize the Scripture quotation in footnotes.</u>

Endnotes

For references and notations not described above—that is, for references that serve more of an *academic* requirement instead of making an interesting note convenient for the reader—I agree it's best to place those in endnotes that appear either at the ends of chapters or at the end of the book.

Placing such notes and references in endnotes saves space on a page containing the narrative. There's no need to take up space on pages with material the majority of your audience definitely won't care about.

— Chapter 15 —

The Big Words

WATCH OUT FOR the *Big* words!

I'm not even using any big words or fancy terms when addressing the issue. I've used this way of talking to authors about "big words" many times simply because this is the way I choose to think of them and because I want the authors to easily remember my admonition.

Certain words used in the wrong place can really get us into trouble not only in writing but also in speaking. At least that's my opinion. You're welcome to think otherwise, but at least hear me out.

What I personally call *Big* words include, *Forever*, *Never*, *Always*, *Nothing*, *All*, *None*, *Every*, *Everything*, *Everyone*, and *No One*. And there are other words I've spoken with authors about, including *Exactly* and *Only*.

I believe it's important for any and all Christian ministers, and any and all Christian writers, to have high standards and make sure some particular words are firmly engraved into our vocabularies with a great deal of understanding.

Big words—and big phrases that we write if we're not careful—can get us into *big trouble*. And that's because the *Big* words are by nature all-encompassing with very restrictive meanings.

When some people form their thoughts and even speak of their spiritual beliefs, they sometimes fail to realize the extent of the meanings of *Big* words. Such failure shows up both in writing and casual conversations; but believe it or not, it can even show up in preaching.

There, I said it.

When we misuse the *Big* words, we open ourselves up to criticism. We can be accused of exaggerating or just plain being in error. And the context in which we misapply the *Big* words will determine how serious our mistake is.

> There really is no room for error when using the *Big* words and phrases if we want to be accurate and respected in what we write.

When we communicate to others, we have an obligation to choose all our words carefully—especially in writing since we actually have more time to think about them. It's not like we're having to pull a word out of our brain at a moment's notice while we're writing. And there *is* in fact a lot of reference material literally available at our fingertips online as we write if we're connected to the internet.

That takes away even more excuses for using the wrong words.

Anytime we're inclined to use any of the *Big* words, it's important to ask ourselves if we really should do it. Their meanings must be satisfied completely.

"Every" means "each and every one" without qualification. "Never" means "never ever, ever." And "all" means "in each and every circumstance you can *ever* think of."

Try to think about this the next time you use a *Big* word.

— Chapter 16 —

Commas

IF WE LOOK back at writing in the not-so-distant past of the twentieth century, we'll find plenty of examples of writers liberally using commas throughout their work—especially in the earlier decades of the 1900s. Commas were so prevalent that it seemed like it must have been a rule to make sure commas get placed in every sentence.

That's not how it is today.

Today it's more accepted (and expected) for writers to use fewer commas in their writing. And because of that, it's probably a good idea for us to pause and consider why commas are used.

> Commas signal pauses and separations within sentences. They're used for separating words or phrases with small pauses to help readers understand what the writer is delivering to them.

Commas are used for two main purposes. First, they're used to increase clarity and ease of reading. And second, they're used to keep people from reading through words. Sometimes if a comma is not placed at a strategic location between words, the reader can understand a sentence to say something that the writer didn't intend it to say.

Getting back to the issue of how things have changed, it seems to me it was once expected of writers to use commas to set off each prepositional phrase in a sentence. But today the emphasis is on smooth, uninterrupted reading. And to me—and evidently to others—that simplifies things. I'm less confused today about when and when not to use commas.

Like other writers, I sometimes have to think about rules and when to use commas. And dealing with that is always part of a proofreading exercise. But it really helps to know that today we have the liberty not to use commas any more than necessary. It helps to be able to put more emphasis on how clearly a sentence reads without them.

Commas in Lists

Commas are used to separate items in lists, such as, "I went to the market to buy apples, oranges, and grapes."

But here's an interesting thing about that comma I placed before the "and." The third comma (the one after "oranges" and preceding the conjunction "and") is called a "*serial* comma" or "*Oxford* comma." The serial comma is always placed before the conjunction introducing the final item in a list.

However, note this: If a writer is following the *AP Style* for using commas, the serial comma isn't used. But if a writer is following the *Chicago Style*, the serial comma IS used.

Now you know why I already gave you some background on style manuals.

There clearly are cases when the context is so clear that following the *AP Style* works just fine. Sometimes there's no confusion caused by leaving out the serial comma. But I've seen many cases when wording and context was not so clear, and the list could easily be misread.

And while the *AP Style* can sometimes cause problems, such isn't the case when the serial comma is applied consistently as stipulated in the *Chicago Manual of Style*. "So why," I ask, "is the *AP Style* of dropping the serial comma even a thing? What purpose does it serve?"

I truly don't know.

And because of that, my advice to you is to always use the serial comma unless you absolutely must follow the style guide of a publisher that has adopted the *AP Style*.

Commas With Conjunctions

One of the things I've seen writer after writer struggle with is when or when not to precede a conjunction in a sentence with a comma. And after all these years I still can't understand why it's so difficult to grasp, but for many it is.

There are several conjunctions, and some of the most common that writers have trouble with are coordinating conjunctions, *and*, *but*, and *for*. The conjunction "and" is the one I deal with most often. So I'll focus on "and" in my discussion.

In addressing this, I'll do my best to make this as simple as I can without placing a lot of focus on terminology.

What we first need to remember about this particular thing is that it's a firmly established grammar rule accepted by pretty much everyone everywhere.

If your personal editor doesn't catch a problem in this area of punctuation (if sometimes a problem slips through), the publisher's copyeditor will likely catch it. But if no one else catches the problem, your readers will, and it won't reflect highly on your abilities as a writer.

Then the second thing to remember is that a complete sentence consists of a subject and a predicate. I know this shouldn't need to be said, but I must. This is where the understanding needs to start.

The subject is a noun or pronoun (a person, place, or thing), and while a predicate can contain other things, it will always contain a *verb* (an action). The subject is the actor (the person, place, or thing that's doing something), and the verb defines what the subject is doing (the action).

> A complete sentence always consists of at least two things—a subject (a noun or pronoun) and a predicate (as simple as a single verb).

Here's a sentence that consists of only two words but is still a complete sentence:

Dogs bark.

"Dogs" is the subject. And "bark" is the verb.

Now let's add something to the sentence—a conjunction. Here's another simple sentence using the conjunction "and":

Dogs bark *and* howl.

Notice there's no comma in the sentence, and this sentence is grammatically correct. The dogs do two things. They bark and howl. There is one subject and two verbs.

Now let's add one more word. Here's the sentence with the word "they" added to the right of the conjunction:

Dogs bark, and *they* howl.

Notice there's now a comma in this sentence.

And I added the comma in this sentence because we added a **subject** (they) **after** the conjunction.

In both the first sentence (Dogs bark) and the second sentence (Dogs bark and howl) there's only one subject— "Dogs" (a plural noun).

In the third sentence there are two subjects—"Dogs" (a plural noun) and "they" (a plural pronoun). And the conjunction (and) is separating them.

So if we evaluate the sentence with the comma, we'll find both a subject (Dogs) and verb (bark) to the **left** of the conjunction as well as both a subject (they) and verb (howl) to the **right** of the conjunction. And since that's the case, a comma is *required* before the conjunction.

That's it!

Regardless of how many words there are in a sentence, to figure out if a comma is needed in front of the conjunction, all we have to do is examine the sentence and see if there's a subject and verb on both sides of the conjunction. If there are, then add the comma. If there aren't don't add the comma.

But there's even a second way you can check to see if using a comma is required. Try to make two sentences out of the statement.

The statement containing a conjunction without the comma was, "Dogs bark and howl." And again, it's a perfectly good statement as far as being grammatically correct.

But here's the result of taking that sentence, using a period, and dropping the conjunction to try to make two sentences out of it:

Dogs bark. Howl.

That of course doesn't make sense. And that's because there's no subject on the right side of the period.

Now look at the statement containing the comma in the sentence, "Dogs bark, and they howl." Let's take that sentence, add a period after "bark," and drop the conjunction to try to make two sentences out of it.

Dogs bark. They howl.

Making two sentences out of that works. And to convert the resulting two sentences back into one sentence again, we basically just replace the period with a comma and put back in the conjunction.

The Rest of the Story

And now . . . the rest of the story.

If you get what I told you above, you don't even need to remember the details and proper grammatical terms I'm about to share with you. It's more important to have the ability to do something than to know or remember terminology that describes it. But in this case, I do think that remembering and understanding two grammatical terms is helpful.

For the record, the terms are, *independent clause* and *dependent clause.*

Considering the sentence, "Dogs bark, and they howl," the phrase, "Dogs bark," is considered an *independent clause.* And it's *independent* because you can make it into a complete sentence by only adding a period after "bark." It can stand alone as a complete sentence because it has all that's required to allow it to exist *independently*—a subject and predicate (verb).

Also, the phrase, "and they howl," is an *independent clause* too, because you can capitalize the "and" (or remove it and capitalize "they") and also make it into a complete sentence standing independently all by itself. "They" is the subject, and "howl" is the predicate (verb).

But considering "Dogs bark and howl," while "Dogs bark" can be turned into a complete, independent sentence to stand alone all by itself, you can't do that with "and howl." So that means the phrase, "and howl," is a *DEPENDENT clause.* And it's called "dependent" because it doesn't have its own subject.

> A clause following a conjunction that contains a verb but does not contain a subject is a *dependent* clause because it *depends* on the subject on the other side of the conjunction for it to be a complete thought. <u>Dependent clauses don't need a comma; they need a *subject.*</u>

There you have it. I hope this helps.

Commas After Conjunctions and First Words in Sentences

Many moons ago my first editor told me something that helped me. And now I'm going to repeat it. If you already know this, you're welcome to skip this and go on to the next section.

As a less-accomplished writer, I was prone to place commas immediately after a number of first words in sentences. I'm talking about sentences beginning like this:

"But, if you . . . "

"And, if you . . .

"Then, if you . . . "

As always, a comma is a *pause signal* to the reader. And we know how useful the short pauses are that commas produce. They add clarity to reading. But when starting a sentence like the examples above, such pauses do *not* bring clarity to reading. Instead, they add emphasis.

Because of its association with the first word of the sentence, such a pause will cause the reader to *hear* or sense the writer's voice, so to speak, as the writer not only pauses but also emphasizes the first word in the statement with a certain virtual voice-like intonation—regardless of whether or not the writer meant to do that.

Writers are generally more prone to using a comma in this position when they're also prone to emphasize those first words in verbal communication.

My editor had to teach me long ago to stop habitually putting commas after the first words in sentences, and if you also habitually put commas after first words in your writing, you too need to end the habit. And here are the reasons.

1. It's habitual.

   If it's indeed habitual, it's not being done for a good reason. It's not being done to bring clarity to your writing. It's not being done to help the reader better receive the message in the sentence. In other words, it's not adding value to your writing. It's simply being done out of habit.

2. It's repetitive.

   Repetition in writing is generally bad unless it's purposeful and somehow presented to the reader as clearly reasonable and sensible. Again, repetition without purpose in writing (and that purpose must be relayed to the reader) is bad, and that includes the overuse of words, phrases, thoughts, sentences, quotations, commas . . . you name it. There's more about repetition coming up in later chapters.

   The fact is, it's not really a problem if a comma is only *occasionally* placed after the first word in a sentence. When it's occasional, it means the writer really does want the reader to pause to notice the writer's emphasis. The pause is intended and important.

   The problem arises when the comma appears too often.

   > Used *occasionally*, inserting a comma
   > after the first word in a sentence is a
   > matter of intentional, planned emphasis.
   > As such, it has value. But used *too much*,
   > it loses value because it's repetitive.

Chapter 17

Colons and Semicolons

BELIEVE IT OR NOT, while not used nearly as often in writing as commas and periods, colons and semicolons deserve their own chapter—that is, deserve to share a chapter. Colons and semicolons are still important punctuation marks, and it won't hurt any of us to refresh our understanding of them.

Some of us have a pretty good feel for when to use colons and semicolons. But perhaps those of us who do a fair job of using them can still get better at it. For beyond doubt, while some writers don't use them when they should—don't use them to their full potential—others overuse them.

Colons (:)

Colons are helpful elements of punctuation when used correctly. But like other elements in writing, they shouldn't be overused. If colons are overused, they'll be seen as *repetitive*. (There's that word again.) The reader can become weary with the overuse of colons and start wondering if the writer knows how to write without them.

The colon has been a strange punctuation mark for ages, and its use has changed over time. I've done my share of reading and updating some books written in the seventeenth century. And I can testify to the changes that have taken place in English since then. One of the things that always struck me as peculiar in those old texts was indeed the use of the colon.

Dealing with so many sentences with colons included in them made both reading and understanding the old books difficult. And the fact that colons were used so liberally back in those days was only half of the problem. The other part of the problem was that it was difficult to understand what rules writers were applying for using them.

Sometimes it appeared the author's use of a colon made sense and aligned more with how we're supposed to use colons today. But often the writer seemed to use a colon as a simple period. (Please don't do that.) And at other times it was impossible to really know what the writers' intentions were.

Looking back now, I'm thinking when it comes to the use of colons in the past, written English was sort of like the *Wild West*—somewhat unorganized and unsettled compared to today. I wonder how people will look at our writing a few hundred years from now.

Today there are limited purposes and fairly broad agreement for using colons. Following is a list of uses for the colon along with some examples.

1. Colons can be used to introduce lists.

    The grocery store had all I needed to prepare the feast: turkey for the main course, potatoes and vegetables, cranberries and oranges for the cranberry salad, and pecans to use for making the pie.

2. Colons can be used to introduce quotations.

    He then spoke those oft-repeated words: "No way, Jose!"

3. Colons can be used before a noun or a noun phrase when completing a statement.

> "She had everything I was looking for in a woman: money."

> (Personally, I would rewrite this using an Em dash: "She had everything I was looking for in a woman—money." More on the dashes, later.)

4. Colons can be used for providing examples or reasons.

> "I hate going camping with him for only one reason: He snores."

5. Colons are used in writing out time, ratios, and references.

> "Your appointment is at 11:15 am."

> "That roof was constructed with a 5:12 pitch."

> *"Jesus wept"* (John 11:35 NKJV).

6. Colons are used to separate titles from subtitles.

> "Have you read the book, *The Masquerade: Deception in the Last Days*, by Donna Sparks?"[7]

> Colons are useful and perfectly fine to use if used sparingly. Just remember that if you or your editor determines there are too many colons in your work, there are other ways to write without colons. So simply limit colons by rewriting.

---

7 *The Masquerade: Deception in the Last Days*, by Donna Sparks, published 2020 by Bridge-Logos.

Semicolons (;)

Before getting into the uses of semicolons, be aware that semicolons are going out of style for *frequent* use. Semicolons are still useful, though, and they aren't about to pass off the scene. They're sometimes still necessary; just keep in mind not to use them any more than you need to.

Like it or not, the overuse of semicolons is increasingly looked upon as evidence of an inexperienced writer or a writer who hasn't kept up with the times and changes in English literature.

Using a Semicolon to Join Two Independent Clauses

Remember our discussion about the use of commas with conjunctions to tie together two independent clauses? The use of a comma and a conjunction can take two clauses that could otherwise stand alone as separate, complete sentences and tie them together into one sentence.

You can look back to Chapter 16 to refresh your memory on using commas.

Well, there's another way to tie together two independent clauses (two complete sentences) into one sentence. To do that the second way, we use a semicolon instead of a comma. And that's usually done by removing both the comma and conjunction and replacing them with a semicolon.

Here's an example of a sentence written with both a comma and a conjunction:

Jesus healed the crippled man, and the crowd was awestruck.

Using a semicolon, it can be written like this:

> Jesus healed the crippled man; the crowd was awestruck.

> Notice that with the semicolon following "the crippled man," the conjunction, *and,* was not needed.

But here's something interesting. It's not always best for reading to delete a conjunction. So if we need to, we can still use the conjunction to introduce an independent clause even when we use a semicolon.

> Here's that simple sentence from the example in Chapter 16:

> Dogs bark, and they howl.

> If we only replace the comma with a semicolon, it looks like this:

> Dogs bark; and they howl.

With this construction, the reading of the two sentences is nearly the same, and grammatically speaking, they're both correctly punctuated. But as I said, these days semicolons shouldn't be used unless they're necessary, so in most cases we should either leave the sentence punctuated with the comma followed by the conjunction or remove the conjunction when using a semicolon.

In the case of our example sentence about dogs, consider the effects of using a semicolon to connect the two independent clauses and removing the conjunction. Here's how it would look.

Dogs bark; they howl.

A conjunction isn't needed when connecting two independent clauses with a semicolon. And using semicolons to join two sentences into one is done mainly to show how two statements are closely related to each other. But when using a semicolon and dropping a conjunction, the resulting sentence still needs to read reasonably well. And this one doesn't.

In this case, "Dogs bark; they howl" doesn't read any better than if we used a period and set them up as two complete sentences. So we should just use a comma and a conjunction to connect them.

> Just because something we write is correct grammatically doesn't mean it's logical, useful, easy to understand, or comfortable to read. Write to be understood first. Just do so using proper grammar.

But let's say we want to take more than two free-standing, complete sentences and join them into one sentence. Following are some options.

Here are three complete sentences:

Dogs are friendly. But they bark. And they also howl.

Here's how to join them together into one sentence with commas:

> Dogs are friendly, but they bark, and they also howl.

Above, they're tied together in one sentence by commas and conjunctions with their capitalization removed.

And here's one option to join them together with semicolons.

> Dogs are friendly; they bark; they also howl.

In this sentence, since conjunctions aren't needed by rule, I dropped both of them. I didn't say the sentence would sound good; that's another issue. But grammatically it's correct. And that's my point.

Now let's try to make it sound better. To do that we'll use a mixture of commas, semicolons, and conjunctions. And there are multiple options.

a. Dogs are friendly, but they bark; they also howl.

b. Dogs are friendly; they bark, and they also howl.

c. Dogs are friendly; but they also bark and howl.

d. Dogs are friendly, but they bark and howl.

If you were choosing one of the above sentences for use in your work, which would you choose? Which seems more natural? Which will sound better in the tone you're setting and within the flow of thought? These are the types of questions you need to consider when writing.

Note that in both of the sentences, c. and d., I removed the subject of the third independent clause ("they"). And after I did that, the third clause became dependent, so a comma was not placed between "bark" and the conjunction ("and").

Note also that making the third clause dependent allowed me to build a sentence with only one comma or one semicolon. That's not a bad thing.

Of course you can switch some words around to build a different sentence. But remember to use proper punctuation between the two types of clauses.

> Dogs bark and howl, but they're friendly.

> Rewriting our work until we get it right is just a good idea.

Using semicolons in lists

Semicolons are sometimes used in lists to either properly punctuate independent clauses in the lists or add clarity for reading.

Example of a List Containing Independent Clauses

> He rented the cabin in the mountains because he wanted to enjoy nature. He sensed his need for rest; he longed for some solitude away from the crowds; and he wanted to get out of the city and breath the fresh mountain air.

In the above example, the only semicolon that could be changed to a comma is the last semicolon in the sentence since that comma would precede a conjunction introducing an independent clause. The other semicolon (after " . . . for rest") is necessary because the next item in the list is an independent clause that doesn't begin with a conjunction.

Example of a List Using Semicolons for Clarity

He has traveled all over the world. Just last year he visited Sydney, Australia; Rome, Italy; Veracruz, Mexico; Berlin, Germany; and Singapore.

Without using semicolons, the sentence would look like this:

He has traveled all over the world. Just last year he visited Sydney, Australia, Rome, Italy, Mexico City, Mexico, Berlin, Germany, and Singapore.

The use of semicolons in some lists definitely improves clarity and readability.

Chapter 18

The Dashes

THERE ARE THREE dashes that you can use in your writing, and all three of the dashes are in fact punctuation marks. The three dashes are the *Hyphen*, the *Em dash*, and the *En dash*.

The Hyphen

The hyphen is the shortest of the three dashes in length, and it's the most common dash used in writing. In fact, it's so common there's a key on every typewriter and computer keyboard assigned to the humble *hyphen*. The hyphen is used for joining words or portions of words together.

Compound Adjectives

Hyphens are commonly seen in words joined together as *compound adjectives*, such as "pet-friendly hotel," "one-of-a-kind automobile," or "well-built house."

Compound Nouns

Hyphens are also commonly seen in words joined together to form *compound nouns*, such as "has-been," "get-togeth-er," "merry-go-round," "six-pack," "great-grandfather," or "runner-up."

But beware, while there are style rules for hyphenating words associated with numbers—such as "five-year-old boy," and, "about three hundred thirty-two million people live in the United States"—and while there's consistency in when compound adjectives are formed, there's little consistency in forming compound nouns.

> Many compound nouns are not hyphenated, and it's pretty much impossible to know or remember all of them that are hyphenated and all of them that are not. So writers should refer to dictionaries when there's any doubt about hyphenating nouns.

The Em Dash

The Em dash is the longest in the dash family. And it's called an Em dash because of its long association with the width of a capital *M*. The Em dash also holds the distinction these days of being the most popular dash following the hyphen.

The popularity of the Em dash has grown because of its flexibility and ability to bring clarity to statements—so much so, that more and more people judge a writer's ability to communicate successfully by his or her successful use of the Em dash.

Using Em Dashes Instead of Parentheses

Em dashes can be used instead of parentheses to set off parenthetical statements. And using Em dashes instead of parentheses not only sometimes increases clarity but also improves emphasis.

But don't use Em dashes for all parenthetical phrases. That can become repetitive. And to maintain clarity, there are times when both a set of parentheses and Em dashes can be used in the same paragraph to enclose separate parenthetical expressions because of the complexity or length of sentences.

Using Em Dashes to Set Off Extra Information

Em dashes are used to set off extra information that's included in sentences for clarification, some of which will contain lists.

Examples:

> The three of them—John, Peter, and Paul—were some of the greatest expounders of God's Word.

> If you need me, let me know—by text message, not phone call—and I'll step out long enough to respond.

Using Em Dashes to Deal with Sentence Fragments

I personally love being able to use Em dashes to set off sentence fragments that I want to use but would be problematic without the dash. An Em dash can be used to set off a fragment that appears either before or following a complete sentence. This is a great way to throw in a thought for effect or feeling without breaking any rules.

Quick interjections into thoughts or statements you want to use but don't want to become wordier than they already are—the Em dash can make quick and clean work of them.

I just gave you an example of that.

Examples:

> Do this, do that, go here, go there—I get tired of people telling me what to do.

"I'm telling you, there's no other way out—at least that I can see."

But beware, because a writer shouldn't continually write in a way that Em dashes show up everywhere on every page of a book. Em dashes, like all other special tools in a writer's toolbox will be effective and natural only when they're not overused.

I've read writers comment on Em dashes and say there shouldn't be more than one or two of them used in one sentence—with two of them enclosing a parenthetical expression or setting off extra information. I agree with that.

But I would go further and say that rarely should there be more than two Em dashes appearing even in one paragraph. Clarity is actually reduced with the use of too many Em dashes. The use of too many of them causes the writing to become visually cluttered and causes confusion.

Even if it starts looking like Em dashes are becoming too visually prominent on a single page, the writer should consider doing some rewriting.

And as somewhat of a restatement, to keep from using Em dashes too often, a writer can always still use parentheses for parenthetical phrases here and there in addition to Em dashes. That will keep down visual clutter. And I make sure I *don't* use Em dashes for all parenthetical statements.

As with other elements of punctuation and the repeated use of words, when it comes to using Em dashes, too much of a good thing is a bad thing.

Additional Points on the Em dash

AP vs. Chicago

There's a difference between the *AP Style* and the *Chicago Style* when it comes to how to use Em dashes. *The AP Stylebook* stipulates the use of a space on both sides of the Em dash to separate it from the words preceding and following the dash.

The *Chicago Manual* stipulates *no spaces* are to be used between the Em dash and the words. When writing books, unless the publisher's style guide requires spaces, follow the recommendation of the *Chicago Manual*.

Since most book publishers adopt *The Chicago Manual of Style*, I make sure the authors I edit employ the *Chicago Style* for Em dashes.

The Em Dash and Independent Clauses

Here's another point I make to the authors I edit: I suggest writers restrain themselves from using Em dashes to separate independent clauses from other independent clauses.

This isn't a rule, but I personally try to use—and encourage others to use—Em dashes only to set off or add emphasis to phrases or fragments that don't contain both subject and verb. Except in rare circumstances, other than for occasional use in setting off parenthetical expressions, I use Em dashes to connect complete sentences to only dependent clauses or sentence fragments.

If this pattern of use is followed, I believe the result is better readability and more consistent use of this form of punctuation throughout the entire manuscript.

The En Dash

The En dash is shorter than an Em dash and longer than a hyphen. It's called an En dash because the length of an En dash is supposed to be the width of a capital *N*. If you look up information on the En dash you'll find it's supposed to be used for separating ranges of numbers—as in "plan to spend 4-6 hours."

The En dash is also used in instances where many of us use a forward slash to denote a relationship between words—as in "a university-corporate partnership" instead of "a university/corporate partnership."

When you read the comments of other writers on the subject of using the En dash in their writing, you'll read that many writers simply ignore the use of an En dash altogether. I personally have never had a publisher or typesetter make an issue out of using hyphens instead of En dashes, but it's still a good thing to know how to use them.

— Chapter 19 —

The Ellipsis . . .

THE ELLIPSIS HAS two main jobs to do in writing. The first job of an ellipsis (with a plural of, "ellipses") is to indicate missing words. The second is to show what may be described as a poignant pause in dialogue or in a writer's narrative. The best advice I can give you on using ellipses in your writing is to limit the use of ellipses to these two uses and use them only when really necessary.

Using an Ellipsis for Missing Words

An ellipsis may be used to replace words at the beginning of a sentence, in the middle of a sentence or group of sentences, or at the end of a sentence. (An ellipsis can signal a very short series of missing words or even many sentences.) Of these three placements, ellipses are most commonly seen in the middle or at the end of a sentence or group of sentences.

There are those who say an ellipsis should never be placed in front of the first word used to introduce a sentence, but I've certainly been guilty of doing that when the formatting seemed to work and it served my purpose—specifically when deleting words from the beginning of quotations.

Like with a lot of other things, in our attempts to get our point across to our readers, we need to focus more on what will be clear to them rather than on strictly satisfying the rules of grammar—unless those rules are the most important ones. (There is that thing called, *Creative License*, but I won't get into that here.)

A mistake in using an ellipsis is certainly not the worst mistake any of us can make in writing. We should, however, do our best to satisfy all the accepted principles in writing if there's no good reason not to.

Here are some examples of the proper use of an ellipsis for showing missing words.

Examples:

> *"For this is how God loved the world: He gave his one and only Son, . . . "* (John 3:16).

> *"God sent his Son into the world . . . to save the world through him"* (John 3:17).

> *" . . . God's light came into the world, but people loved the darkness more than the light, for their actions were evil"* (John 3:19).

Using an Ellipsis for Trailing off a Thought

An ellipsis may be used to trail off a thought in dialogue to indicate someone's statement is interrupted.

Example:

> "You know I've told you a thousand times that . . . "
> "Now just a minute!" He shot back and didn't let her continue the diatribe.

Using an Ellipsis for a Pause in a Statement

Although I suggest you keep this use of the ellipsis to a bare minimum, ellipses may be used to indicate special pauses in statements either in the author's narrative or in dialogue.

Example:

> I opened up my laptop computer and placed it before me on my legs as I sat on my duff in my recliner and began to write . . . er . . . type. (This is from this book's introduction.)

The Proper Form of an Ellipsis

When looking into how we should properly form an ellipsis, we'll find that once again there is disagreement between the two most influential style guides. *The AP Stylebook* stipulates ellipses are to be formed with three consecutive periods, like this:

> So . . . how'd it go? (Use a space, dot, dot, dot, space.)

But *The Chicago Manual of Style* stipulates we should do it like this:

> So . . . how'd it go? (Use a space, dot, space, dot, space, dot, space.)

So . . . how should *you* do it? Just like I did it. follow the *Chicago Manual* unless told otherwise by your publisher.

The Ellipsis in Word Processing Software

I can't speak to the current state of other word processing software, but I know that in both Microsoft Word and Open Office by Apache, if you type three periods in a row, they will automatically replace those three periods with an "ellipsis" symbol. And the ellipsis symbol in those two applications is a symbol that reflects the *AP Style*.

Unless you're told to use the *AP Style* in your writing—if you're guilty of typing three periods in a row and letting your word processor insert an *AP Style* ellipsis symbol into your work—please give your editor a break. Stop doing that and type space, dot, space, dot, space, dot, space. I'm not suggesting you do anything more than what my editor told me to do many years ago.

— Chapter 20 —

Syntax

THE WORD "SYNTAX" refers to an orderly system of connecting things together. When it comes to writing, *syntax* basically refers to how words are used, grouped together, and organized, or ordered, to make statements the reader will understand.

The proper use of syntax in writing can be a big subject to address, and the purpose of this chapter is by no means to exhaust the subject and explain extensively how words are to be used, ordered, and organized. It's simply my purpose here to get the writer to think about it and consider how proper syntax is important.

A Syntax Summary

Employing proper syntax in our writing is tantamount to properly using words, employing proper word order, and satisfying accepted rules of grammar, such as correctly addressing subject-verb agreement or the best placement of direct and indirect objects. But it's not limited to only that. Proper syntax covers many things.

The Choice and Position of a Word

The mere choice of a word is important, and editors occasionally find themselves letting writers know that the word they've used isn't the right one. Sometimes a chosen word doesn't align with what the writer is thinking or intending to say.

> Sometimes even if a word seems right, it may not be the right word to use in a particular context because it has a shade of meaning that the writer has not considered.
> Words can be funny things.

But even when we choose the *right word*, if we place it in the *wrong position* in a phrase or sentence, it can change the message. Just the position of the word can have the writer saying something he or she really didn't intend to say. That's a *Syntax* issue.

Examples of How Word Position Affects Things

1. "*Only* Dave drinks water."

   This tells us Dave is the only one who drinks water. No one else drinks water—only Dave.

2. "Dave *only* drinks water."

   Dave doesn't swim in water or wash his hands with it. He only drinks it.

3. "Dave drinks *only* water."

   Dave doesn't drink coffee, tea, juice, or broth. He drinks only water.

So which word placement above tells the real story? One is clearly closer to the truth than the other two, but to understand it, we need something else.

To determine whether or not we're using the proper syntax in the word order, the "something else" we need to know is *context,* and no context was given to us in the above examples. It's the context within which words and phrases are used and ordered that clarifies many things.

Noun-Pronoun Agreement

Believe it or not, it's actually important for nouns and pronouns to agree. And all writers—inexperienced writers, experienced writers, editors, newbies, oldies, whoever—have to consciously proof their work to make sure they are in fact in agreement. This also is a syntax issue.

> Noun-Pronoun Agreement goes beyond agreement in gender and means every pronoun used to refer to a noun or another pronoun must be in agreement in number —as to being either singular or plural.

I won't spend much time dealing with this in a general way, because anyone who writes should have a pretty good understanding of this. However, in a specific way I *will* address one concern I have on this topic that's causing a lot of trouble for writers today.

I feel so strongly about what I'm about to address that I'm not presenting it to you as a subsection, or subtask in dealing with noun-pronoun agreement. I'm elevating it to its own section.

Politically Correct Writing and Gender Warriors

A trend has appeared in writing—seemingly across every discipline—and that trend seems to have become a *caving-in* to negative forces as not only our nation but also the world continues its furious march toward losing grip on gender identity.

In that march, the furore is fueled by those who use everything at their disposal—the broadcast media, social media, politics, religion, indoctrination within classrooms, and on an on—to change society and its morals to suit them.

As that relates to those of us who write, I want you to not only consider the attempts of many to rid the English language of any vestige of what they call sexist discrimination but also the work of writers who appear to be following their lead like bleating sheep.

At the forefront of the struggle that's spilled over into a war on the English language is a battle over the use of the words *he, him,* and *his.*

He, Him, and His

In English grammar, the words *he, him,* and *his* are masculine pronouns, but that's the case only when *context* proves that true. While *she, her,* and *hers* are always feminine pronouns, if context doesn't prove *he, him,* and *his* are to be understood as masculine, they're gender-neutral pronouns.

In other words, if context doesn't clearly reveal that *he* is referring to a man or male of a species in the animal world, *he* always means either "he or she"—basically, a being. For a very, very long time, English speakers have done just fine with that and have not lived in confusion over it at all. But now the anti-sexist warriors won't stand for it. They reject historical order and promote confusion.

I'm tempted to think, "Okay, so if you like, we can switch the rule of English around and make '*her*' gender neutral.

I've spent my whole life living with a pronoun that's shared with another gender (or lack of one), and *she* doesn't have to share her pronoun with anyone!"

OK, OK . . . but getting to the bottom line of what I want to address, the main problem to me is not that anti-sexist warriors are fighting, it's that all too many writers (many Christians included) are caving into their pressure. They're yielding to them by prioritizing being politically correct over being accurate in their writing.

To keep from offending anti-sexist elitists, writers are *purposely* producing work that introduces confusion. It's now becoming a fairly common thing to see some writers purposely break truly important rules of English grammar only because they don't want to hurt the feelings of those who want to not only ruin our society but also change our language in the process.

Yes, that's my editorial opinion.

To be specific, I'm talking about writers using the words *they*, *them*, and *their* as a substitute for *he*, *him*, and *his*.

They, Them, and Their

They, *them*, and *their* are plural pronouns, and to honor the English language we should continue to respect that fact. In my opinion, writers of English everywhere should rise up and tell the world, "If you don't like us using *he*, *him*, and *his* as gender-neutral singular pronouns, then give us new gender-neutral pronouns; don't bastardize the English language by messing up the difference between singular and plural."

By the way, if you don't think this has become a problem, I'll give you an example that should send shivers down your back as a Christian. And be warned, I'm shifting into preacher mode again.

I believe the editors of the *New International Version* of the Bible consciously and purposely changed Scripture to reflect either a fear of or support for radical, misguided, anti-sexist warriors—some of whom would love to get rid of the Bible altogether.

Following are examples of wording from the newest edition of the NIV (2011) compared to wording in the NKJV and NLT.

Then Jesus said to his disciples, "Whoever wants to be my disciple must deny themselves and take up their cross and follow me."   (Matthew 16:24 <u>NIV</u>)

Then Jesus said to His disciples, "If anyone desires to come after Me, let him deny himself, and take up his cross, and follow Me."   (Matthew 16:24 <u>NKJV</u>)

Then Jesus said to his disciples, "If any of you wants to be my follower, you must give up your own way, take up your cross, and follow me."   (Matthew 16:24 <u>NLT</u>)

In the above example, the translators and editors of the NIV used the singular pronoun, "Whoever," and followed it by referring to that singular person as "themselves" and "their."

Let no one in the field go back to get their cloak.   (Matthew 24:18 <u>NIV</u>)

And let him who is in the field not go back to get his clothes.   (Matthew 24:18 <u>NKJV</u>)

> *A person out in the field must not return even to get*
> *a coat.* (Matthew 24:18 <u>NLT</u>)

In this example, the translators and editors of the NIV used the singular, "no one," and followed it by referring to that singular person as "their."

Further, note in both of the above examples that they're dealing with the words of Jesus. Does any reasonable person think if Jesus were speaking or writing to us today in English that He would be confused about noun-pronoun agreement? The NIV translators and editors are not only willingly and purposely misusing English grammar, they are doing it at the expense of casting shade over Jesus' abilities to properly communicate in English.

> *Remember this: Whoever turns a sinner from the error*
> *of their way will save them from death and cover over a*
> *multitude of sins.* (James 5:20 <u>NIV</u>)

> *Let him know that he who turns a sinner from the error of*
> *his way will save a soul from death and cover a multitude*
> *of sins.* (James 5:20 <u>NKJV</u>)

> *You can be sure that whoever brings the sinner back from*
> *wandering will save that person from death and bring*
> *about the forgiveness of many sins.* (James 5:20 <u>NLT</u>)

In the above example, the translators and editors of the NIV used the singular noun, "sinner," and followed that by referring to one sinner as "their" and "them."

Each one should test their own actions. Then they can take pride in themselves alone, without comparing themselves to someone else. (Galatians 6:4 <u>NIV</u>)

But let each one examine his own work, and then he will have rejoicing in himself alone, and not in another. (Galatians 6:4 <u>NKJV</u>)

Pay careful attention to your own work, for then you'll get the satisfaction of a job well done, and you won't need to compare yourself to anyone else. (Galatians 6:4 <u>NLT</u>)

In this example, the translators and editors of the NIV used the singular "Each one," and followed it by referring to that singular person as "their," "they," and "themselves."

Summing Up My Point

Here are some facts to consider:

In these examples, I highlighted nouns and pronouns that should be in agreement in the *New International Version* but are not. And I used Scriptures from multiple books of the Bible.

Genuine Bible translation work is done by committees, not one person. Multiple editors and translators are assigned to individual books of the Bible, and they all check the work. Each word of each verse of each chapter of each book of the Bible is proofed by multiple people over and over.

I'm saying this because I want you to realize the decision to break a very basic rule of grammar for the sake of being politically correct in the latest version of the NIV was a decision purposely made *by committee* and applied to the entire project of updating the NIV in 2011. The previous edition of the NIV published in 2004 doesn't depart from the proper use of either singular or plural pronouns.

Further, what I quoted are merely small samplings of a huge number of instances of purposely mishandling English grammar in the NIV for a worldly political agenda. And I think it's pathetic that translators, editors, and theologians would decide to do that—especially to the Bible.

I find their decision to change wording in the Bible to merely suit the feelings and desires of people—anyone— today not just distasteful but insidious, and it causes me to distrust their efforts to the point that I refuse to use any Scripture from the NIV newer than the 2004 edition.

OK, enough preaching—now let's get into what I believe is a decent solution to deal with the issue in our writing.

A Solution for Addressing Gender

As a writer and a minister, I understand accommodating readers from many backgrounds if possible without compromising Scripture. And when it's not necessary to take a stand that disturbs people (as in not picking a fight when it's not necessary), I have no problem with a writer taking steps to keep from offending the sensibilities of readers.

But I also see a need for the steps we take to be logical with some hope that they'll be approved by God. I see no problem at all in finding a proper and workable solution to keep from having to use *he*, *him*, and *his* as gender-neutral pronouns. So let's look at options. And I'll end with an option I prefer until someone gives us new pronouns for English.

One way to deal with "him" when looking for a gender-neutral singular replacement is to write "him or her." And sometimes I do that, but not continually. I do it occasionally if the sentence reads comfortably. But I know if I do it too often it's going to get repetitive and annoying, so I want a better solution to use more often.

Before telling you what I think is one of the best solutions that I implement in my own writing—and suggest often in editing—I want to draw your attention back to the previous examples of Scripture quotations.

You'll see in them that I included Scripture verses from both the *New King James Version* and the *New Living Translation* for comparing against the NIV. I won't get into discussing any controversy over how the NLT translators and editors dealt with translating Scripture, but I will point out that they avoided conflicts between singular nouns and attempts to find a gender-neutral word to match by rewriting the passage in such a way that it became unnecessary.

So leading up to my solution and forming the foundation for it, if you don't want to use *he*, *him*, or *his*, consider rewriting your sentences so it's not necessary.

> Here is my favorite solution for the pronoun gender-dilemma: Rewrite the sentence with all plural nouns and pronouns.

I rewrite lots of sentences to keep from using singular pronouns. If you consistently see if you can write in plural instead of singular, there will no longer be a temptation to break one of the more important rules of grammar and write something that looks so (as it truly is) awful.

Following are some simple examples of what I mean.

As hypothetically delivered to me for editing:

Believe me, anyone who understands their responsibility to love one another will put a watchman at the door of their mouth.

Above, "anyone" is singular; so the pronouns referring back to "anyone" must therefore also be singular, but they're not. So there's work to do on this sentence. Here are three options for correcting the syntax:

Option One (traditional English):

Believe me, anyone who understands his responsibility to love others will put a watchman at the door of his mouth.

Note: This is a perfectly good sentence because, in context, "his" is gender-neutral. That said, if this were in a book written by a woman specifically for women readers, I suggest it could be logical to change "his" to "her."

Option Two (to be inclusive—or as they say, less sexist):

Believe me, anyone who understands his or her responsibility to love others will put a watchman at the door of his or her mouth.

Note: I reject the second option because of the repeated "his or her."

Option Three (how I edited it):

Believe me, people who understand their responsibilities to love one another will put a watchman at the door of their mouths.

> Note: I accepted the plural "their" and changed other words from singular to plural.

The moral of this story is that if you'll write more in plural instead of singular, you'll be able to more easily avoid dealing with gender.

Direct Objects, Indirect Objects, and Their Placement

> WARNING: This is one of the more tedious sections in this book. But for those who have this stuff down pat, please tolerate it for the sake of those who need and will benefit from it.

Direct Object

A direct object is a noun, pronoun, or noun phrase that receives the action of a verb (is acted upon).

Example:

Then Jesus broke the <u>bread</u>.

In the above example "Jesus" is the subject; "broke" is the verb, and "bread" is the direct object. Jesus is the one who initiated the action. The action performed was the breaking. And the bread received the action of the breaking.

Indirect Object

An indirect object is the *beneficiary* of the action—to whom or for whom the action was done.

Example:

Then Jesus broke the bread for the <u>disciples</u> to eat.

In this example, the subject (Jesus) performed an action (broke). The direct object (the bread) received the action. And Jesus broke it *for* the disciples (the indirect object—the beneficiaries of the action).

It's probably good to note here that just as there can be multiple subjects and verbs in sentences, there can also be multiple direct objects and multiple indirect objects. It all depends on how the writer decides to structure sentences to present thoughts to the reader.

Example:

> Then Jesus <u>broke</u> the <u>bread</u> and <u>gave</u> <u>it</u> to the <u>disciples</u> to eat.

In this example there are two verbs and two direct objects but only one indirect object. The subject (Jesus) performed two actions. He "broke" (the first verb) and "gave" (the second verb). The first direct object (bread) was the first object acted upon, and the second direct object (it) was the second object acted upon.

The "disciples" became the indirect object in the second clause in the sentence (a dependent clause) when they became the beneficiary of the action (the giving of "it").

Following are some more examples of using direct objects and indirect objects starting once again with a basic sentence structure and moving on from there.

Sentence Structure and Word Order

1. A complete sentence can lack an object—contain only *subject* and *verb*.

   Example:

   The <u>farmer</u> <u>planted</u>.

2. A sentence can have multiple *direct objects* even when there's only one subject and verb.

   Example:

   The farmer planted <u>corn</u>, <u>potatoes</u>, and <u>beans</u>.

3. A sentence can have multiple direct objects with only one *indirect object*.

   Example:

   The farmer sold corn, potatoes, and beans to <u>the man</u>.

4. A sentence can have only one direct object with *multiple indirect objects*.

   Example:

   The farmer sold corn to <u>the man</u> and also to <u>the woman</u>.

5. A sentence can have multiple subjects, multiple verbs, multiple objects, and multiple indirect objects. And I'll note that the following example sentence is constructed in a way that its reading is both logical and smooth. In other words, it demonstrates good syntax.

Example:

$$\text{s.} \quad \text{v.} \quad \text{d.o.} \quad \text{i.o.}$$

The <u>farmer</u> <u>sold</u> <u>corn</u> to <u>the man</u>, and the

$$\text{s.} \quad \text{v.} \quad \text{d.o.} \quad \text{i.o.}$$

<u>farmer's wife</u> <u>made</u> <u>tea</u> for <u>the man</u> and his

$$\text{i.o.}$$

<u>children</u>

The Order of Objects and Indirect Objects

Although indirect objects commonly follow their related direct objects, indirect objects can also precede the objects. The order is up to the writer.

NOTE: The following example is written to prove a point. I'm not saying this is the best way to write the sentence. It's grammatically accurate, but as far as syntax goes, it needs improvement.

Example:

$$\text{s.} \quad \text{v.} \quad \text{i.o.} \quad \text{d.o.}$$

The <u>farmer</u> <u>sold</u> <u>the man</u> <u>corn</u>; and for both

$$\text{i.o.} \quad \text{i.o.} \quad \text{s.}$$

<u>the man</u> and his <u>children</u>, the <u>farmer's wife</u>

$$\text{v.} \quad \text{d.o.}$$

<u>made</u> <u>tea</u>.

As a bonus here, note that I used a semicolon after the first independent clause instead of a comma.

"The father sold the man corn; and . . .."

It only needs to be a comma by rule, but in this instance a semicolon is helpful to keep the reader from reading through the "and" in anticipation of something else the farmer sold in addition to corn. The semicolon is used to make doubly sure the reader pauses.

> Beyond writing for accuracy, when choosing
> word order (for proper or improved syntax)
> always try to write for comfortable
> reading and optimal clarity.

Chapter 21

This and That

THE WORK OF many writers will improve when they gain from experience the ability to consistently manage time and place. Proper management of time and place is important in keeping the mind of the reader where it should be until it's time to move somewhere else in the narrative or story.

We'll deal with "time" in more detail in Chapter 26. But the issue of both time and place will be our focus in this chapter as we discuss the words, "this" and "that," as well as their plurals, "these" and "those."

The Use of "This"

Many writers misuse the word "this" as a pronoun when writing about people, places, or things. It's common when I'm editing a manuscript to correct the use of "this" and change it to "that." As I see it, there are two reasons for the writer's tendency to use "this" as the first choice.

First, I believe writers tend to think of "this" first because the thing they're describing or telling the reader about is right there in their minds in the present even if they're writing about something in the past or not in their possession. It's what the writer is thinking about, so "this" seems logical.

Second, no one has told the writers they should do otherwise.

> The ability of the writer to understand and
> properly choose between "this" and "that"
> to control time and place for the reader
> is at least in part related to the writer's
> ability to view his or her writing from
> the perspective of the reader.

I allude to the writer's ability to view the writer's work from the perspective of the reader, or writing for the reader, several times in this book—even at the risk of sounding repetitive. But it's repeated only because it's related to so many issues. It's that important!

When to Use "This"

When you're writing about something with you or in your possession at the moment you're writing about it, use the word, *this*. And to be clear, "this" speaks of something with you in the present, not something that was with you at a time in the past.

Think of "this" as being something you're holding in your hand or looking at right in front of you or beside you.

When using "this," we're saying something like, "*this* thing here," "*this* thing we're presently discussing," or, "*this* thing before me on my desk."

The same holds true when using the plural of "this"— *these*. Think of *these things* as being both in the present and with you or in your possession as you write.

The Use of "That"

The word, "that," is a pretty flexible word in English. It can function as an adjective: "It's not this thing it's *that* thing." It can function as a conjunction: "I sat down in the easy chair *that* was calling my name." It can also function as an adverb: "The nap I took was about *that* long." And it can function as a pronoun: "*That* is the chair I nap in." There's more on the uses of *that* in the following two chapters. (I like chairs and naps.)

But instead of getting wrapped up in having to figure out what part of speech *that* is here, let's just think of it as referring to something *that* is not with us. A "that" is not with us now even though it may have been with us in the past. And "that" is not in our possession as we write about it.

For the sake of clarifying the difference between using "this" and "that," let's digress for a moment and take another look at "this." Think about *this* for a moment. If we're speaking of something in the past or even in the present, but it's in the next county, it wouldn't be natural for us to write, "*This* is not in my possession; I lost it last year," or, "*This* is not in my possession; it's in Logan County."

The natural ways to write those statements are, "*That* is not in my possession; I lost it last year," and, "*That* is not in my possession; it's in Logan County." *That* will make more sense to the reader.

The difference between when to use "this" and when to use "that" becomes apparent once a person gets used to the concept of making sure our writing should differentiate between them. But sometimes there's only a fine difference between them, and a writer needs to really consider it before making the decision to use one or the other.

Hopefully *this* will help:

When to Use "That"

1. Use *that* when you're writing about something that's *not* with you or in your possession when you write about it.

Think of "that" as being something that you're *not* holding in your hand or looking at with it right in front of you or beside you. Think of "that" as something on the other side of the room. When using "that," we're saying something like, "*that* thing over there," or "*that* thing on *your* desk."

That thing is somewhere else or in someone else's possession.

2. Use *that* when you're writing about something in the past.

> If you're writing about something *that* existed
> or happened in the past, keep it in the past
> instead of bringing it into the present
> with "this." Consistently use "that"
> to refer to things in the past.

When speaking of things in the past, we'll say something like, "*that* thing back there," or, "*that* thing back then that I'm talking to you about now." Basically, "that thing" in the past is no longer in anyone's possession now or anywhere in the present, so don't refer to it as "this thing."

These and Those

What holds true for the singular holds true for the plural.

When using the plural of "this"—*these*—think of *these things* as being both in the present and with you or in your possession as you write.

When using the plural of "that"—*those*—think of *those things* as being either in the past or *not* with you or in your possession as you write.

The Option of Using Neither This Nor That

If you arrive at a point where it's not clear to you which word to use—whether *this* or *that*—another option would be to rewrite the sentence so neither is necessary.

Example: Instead of writing something like,

This issue always bothered me.

Replace it with,

The issue always bothered me.

Chapter 22

That and Which

THIS CHAPTER FOCUSES on using "that" as a conjunction. We'll primarily deal with when "that" can be used as a conjunction and when it can't. And "when it can't" is directly related to the proper use of the word "which"—that is, related to the difference between how the two words are used.

The General Use of That

Before getting into the difference between *that* and *which*, though, let's first discuss the most common use of the word *that*—or rather its overuse. It's actually common for writers to use too many instances of *that* in their work, and it can and does sometimes become a real issue that needs corrected.

There's no doubt about it; writing *that* in a sentence is in many cases not necessary. When it's not necessary to bring understanding to what's written, the word *that* is superfluous—not needed. And used too often it's simply repetitive, and as such, the overuse of *that* can reflect poorly on the writer's experience.

There are those who are adamant about not using *that* unless it's absolutely necessary. And on the extreme end of the scale are those who criticize every use of the word as a conjunction except for very restrictive purposes.

I land on the side of those who think we should definitely examine our sentences and remove occurrences of *that* when it's clearly superfluous but keep it if it helps bring clarity to reading the sentence or keeps the reader from misunderstanding the statement—even at the cost of sometimes sounding superfluous to the "that" connoisseurs.

In other words, in editing I'll remove occurrences of "that" when I believe no reader will need them, but I'll leave in a "that" (and sometimes even add one) when I think it will help the reader—make reading more comfortable or more natural.

> Watch out for using too many "thats" in sentences. Remove them if they're clearly not needed by the reader. And use your best judgment to determine when you think it will be helpful to leave one in.

The Difference between That and Which

There's often an important grammatical difference between the words, "that" and "which." The problem is, far too few people seem to know it. And to tell you the truth, I suppose there are a whole lot of people who not only don't know the difference but also don't care. But that shouldn't be true of a writer.

Knowing when to use "that" as a conjunction to join two phrases and when to use "which" to join them is important for good writers to understand. And that's because, while plenty of people don't know about the difference, there are a lot of readers who do.

The Which Hunt

My first editor, David A. Womack, taught me to go on what he called a "Which Hunt." The word *which* is often misused in sentences when the writer should've instead used the word *that*. You see, it's not only "that" we should know as being capable of overuse.

After reading about this, it seems long ago in an era now past and long forgotten, the words *that* and *which* were largely interchangeable. (Wow! This is sounding like a great movie intro.) However, things changed. For a long time now the two words have been used to show either a *dependency* between two phrases (in the case of "that") and a certain *independence* between two phrases (in the case of "which").

In English grammar, the difference between the two words is shown by describing how they work with two types of clauses—the *restrictive clause* and the *nonrestrictive clause*.

The Use of "That" (for restrictive clauses)

According to *Merriam-Webster*, which is a pretty good source of information, "a restrictive clause is a part of a sentence that may not be removed without rendering that sentence incomplete, difficult to understand, or with its meaning substantially changed."[8]

> NOTE: The phrase above starting with "which," that follows the comma ("which is a pretty good source of information"), is a classic example of a *nonrestrictive* clause. It's added information that's not necessary for understanding the primary message of the sentence.

The word, "that," is used to connect a *restrictive* clause—"a part of a sentence that may not be removed"—to the other part of the sentence.

---

8   https://www.merriam-webster.com/words-at-play/when-to-use-that-and-which, accessed January 30, 2023.

Here's a sentence that contains a restrictive clause connected to the rest of the sentence with "that" as a conjunction.

Example:

> The pastor's car that broke down on the side of the road needs a new transmission.

The clause being *restricted* in this sentence by "that" is the phrase, "broke down on the side of the road."

The clause is *restrictive* because it describes the pastor's car beyond the fact that it needs a new transmission. It's restrictive because it's needed to further identify the car the writer is talking about. Let's write a little dialogue to help this sink in.

> "Which car needs a transmission?" she asked.
>
> "It's the pastor's car," he answered.
>
> "Which car? He has two."
>
> "It's the one that broke down on the side of the road yesterday."

You see, by using the word "that" as a conjunction to connect the two phrases, the writer signaled to us we had to know it was the car that broke down on the side of the road that needs a new transmission. It wasn't any other car. If the pastor had two cars, it wasn't the pastor's other car that was perhaps safely tucked away in his garage.

Also note—**and this is important**—when "that" is used to introduce a restrictive clause, there is *no comma* placed before the "that."

The Use of "Which" (for nonrestrictive clauses)

Unlike a restrictive clause (a statement that's necessary to fully understand the message the writer is relaying to us), a *nonrestrictive* clause simply gives us additional information. And without that information the sentence still gives us all the information we really need when it comes to the primary thing the writer wants us to know.

Example:

> The pastor's car, which broke down on the side of the road, needs a new transmission.

In this example, since the phrase "broke down on the side of the road" started with the word, "which," the writer signaled to us that the clause it introduces is *nonrestrictive*. And that basically means the information isn't actually necessary. We can remove it and still fully grasp the main thing the writer wanted us to know.

The nonrestrictive clause isn't needed and merely gives us additional information that's interesting. The main message the writer wanted to relay to us is simply, "The pastor's car needs a new transmission."

Note that the nonrestrictive clause is set off from the rest of the sentence not only by the word "which" but also by placing *a comma before "which."* The comma puts a short pause there in the reading that also helps us understand the following clause is providing us additional information not really needed to understand the main point of the sentence.

Now let's write a little dialogue to illustrate what we're talking about here.

"Which car needs a transmission?" she asked.

"It's the pastor's car," he answered.

"Oh."

"Yeah, he said it broke down on the side of the road yesterday."

> "Which" makes the phrase it introduces unnecessary. You can take it out because it's *additional* information.
>
> "That" makes the phrase it introduces necessary. You can't take it out because it's *needed* information.

But as is the case in all too many instances, writers—being the people we are—just can't seem to leave well enough alone. So eventually, what's proper and sometimes perfectly understandable at one time can get less so over the years. Make sure to read the following section to find out more about the *That and Which* issue.

That vs. Which—Where to Err

Of note here is that, among others, *Merriam-Webster* acknowledges that in prose (non-poetic work), by the end of the twentieth century the words *that* and *which* have become fairly interchangeable in *American* English when used for introducing restrictive clauses.

And in the case of using "which" to introduce a restrictive clause, it's merely the **lack** of the comma in front of "which" that actually signals the fact it is indeed restrictive and is not meant to be extra, unnecessary information.

But after saying all of that, if you research this in *The Chicago Manual of Style*, you'll find that the *Chicago* gurus don't exactly appreciate *Merriam-Webster's* comments on using "which" for restrictive clauses (even though they still recommend writers use the *Merriam-Webster Collegiate Dictionary*). They point out that dictionaries record common usage of words and are NOT the authority on how words **should** be used.

> Bottom Line: For consistency and to stay in agreement with the *Chicago Style*, all *restrictive* clauses should still always be introduced with no comma and *that*.

Wouldn't it be nice if written English weren't such a challenge and we could all just get along? Well, don't get your hopes up.

There's no worldwide committee that sits down to determine the rules of English. There never has been, and there isn't one now. The English language continues to change, and accepted methods of writing continue to change. Outside of the most stringent rules that apply to the very basics of how we communicate, rules can change over time, because they're generally made up to acknowledge how the majority of writers come to write.

I suppose you didn't know you have such power at your fingertips. Stay humble.

Keeping that in mind, you and I still have some say in how we choose to express ourselves. Up to a point, there's nothing wrong with us using our own creativity and following our own preferences in writing to express ourselves as long as we can be understood by our readers—and, of course, as long as our preferences and styles are accepted by those to whom we answer (those like editors and publishers).

I feel so special right now.

That said, my choice on the use of *that* and *which* is to **not** agree the words, "that" and "which," are interchangeable to introduce restrictive clauses. I'll stick with the folks in Chicago.

> If I appear to anyone to err on this matter, I'll err on the side of clarity and limiting confusion. I'll continue the practice of going on a "Which Hunt" in every piece I write and edit. "That" is restrictive. "Which" is not.

— Chapter 23 —

That and Who

THIS IS ONE of the shortest chapters in the book. And that's because it won't take me much time to pass along the difference between "that" and "who." But I don't want to give you the impression I don't think this is important. This chapter is about using the word *that* as a pronoun.

The Correct Use of "That" as a Pronoun

Simply put, use "that" as a pronoun to refer to *places or things*.

Use *that* or *there* to refer to places regardless of where they are, unless they're so close to you that you can use *this* or *here*—referring to where you actually are.

Use *that* to refer to *inanimate objects*.

Use *that* to refer to *animals* or *insects*.

The Correct Use of Who (which is *always* a pronoun)

Use **who** to refer to people. It's as simple as *that*.

Summing Up My Point

Hopefully this is pretty easy to grasp. Clearly though, not enough writers think about the difference between "that" and "who" as pronouns. I quite often correct the use of "that" when it's used to refer to people.

When speaking of people, it's not "the man *that* did so and so." It's "the man *who* did so and so." It's "the people who . . . " not "the people that . . .."

Maintaining a strict difference between "that" and "who" is my unyielding preference as an editor. It just makes sense. And if you follow my advice, you'll be able to maintain consistency in your writing when referring to people, places, and things.

> I always use "who" as well as all the masculine and feminine pronouns when referring to people to honor the difference between mankind and all other parts of Creation. But I also do it to honor our creator, **who** made us in His image. God is NOT a "that."

I make an exception to my rule on pronouns referring to insects and animals. I use gender-specific pronouns to refer to animals and insects *when* their gender is known. (He's a good dog;" or "She's a good dog.")

Besides the use of the other pronouns,

- Use ***that, it,*** *they, they're, them, these, those,* and *their* when referring to ***non-human things***.

- Use ***who, whom,*** *they, they're, them, these, those,* and *their* when referring to ***human beings and God*** (with only singular "who" and "whom" used to refer to God, the Father, the Holy Spirit, the "Son," or "Jesus" unless using "they," "they're," "them," and "their" to refer specifically to multiple persons within the Trinity).

> No one will be able to fault you for consistency unless you're consistently wrong.

— Chapter 24 —

Repetition

ONE OF THE worst things you can be as a writer is *repetitive*. Repetition can kill otherwise good writing. Readers notice repetition, and they aren't usually amused by it. And depending on what kind of repetition they're faced with, it can actually offend their intelligence.

We must proof our writing for repetition and *consciously* give our readers credit for being able to read and understand the first occurrences of the things we write. We need to write with the assumption that readers have the ability to remember what we wrote.

When it comes to even the simpler things we're prone to repeat—words, instead of complete thoughts—most readers will just become annoyed by repetition. But if they get enough annoyed, they may quit reading.

All that said, don't get down in the dumps if you're guilty of inadvertently putting repetition into your work. Just determine to address it. Even the most skilled writers have to deal with tendencies to be repetitious. Even the best writers have to be careful not to repeat too often their favorite words, phrases, or expressions.

What you have to share is worth writing about, and if God is calling you to write, then God will give you the things you need to get it done. Hopefully, one of those things is an experienced editor as a partner. Am I being repetitive here?

And be mindful of this: If your editor continues to point out repetition in your work and says you need to address it, you'll benefit by accepting the editor's admonition with a teachable spirit. You'll profit by actively and intentionally dealing with the issue.

> One of the big differences between poor writers and good writers is that good writers learn to recognize and acknowledge their weaknesses or bad habits in writing and intentionally take steps to address them.

Dealing With Unplanned Repetition

We learn from problems when we go beyond recognizing them to actually dealing with them—even in writing. We won't learn from problems when we ignore them after they're brought to our attention.

Sorry, but it's true. People can learn when people want to learn. People can take action when people want to take action. As one of my former pastors, Ron McCaslin, Senior Pastor Emeritus of Spring Creek Assembly of God in Edmond, Oklahoma, said from the pulpit—not often but occasionally and just enough—when it comes to doing what we should,

"It's not a matter of can or can't; it's a matter of will or won't."

I believe that definitely applies to learning. Believe me, even the best of Christian writers had to learn to write well. And the best Christian writers are still learning.

If you have a habit of using a word or phrase over and over again to the point of wearing it out, recognize it, admit it, and deal with it. And if you have a habit of being repetitive in the use of added emphasis—like overusing italics, words in all-caps, or exclamation points—recognize it, admit it, and deal with it. (There's more on this in the next chapter.)

Repetition With a Purpose

Unnecessary and unplanned repetition that we unconsciously or habitually put into our writing needs to be caught and edited out of our work when we proof. But there are times when we *want* to repeat something with good reason to remind the reader of something or reinforce it.

There are other times when we want to repeat something for the sake of perhaps making yet another point with it. In those cases we just need to be careful how we present the repetition.

When using purposeful repetition, we need to let the reader know in some way that we realize we're repeating something; we're doing it intentionally, and we have a purpose for it.

To signal to the writer that we actually know we're repeating something, we may write something like, "In chapter ten I spoke of . . . ," or, "Remember, I said . . . ," or, "To repeat . . . ," or, "Let's consider again that . . . ."

If you've been keeping track of the repetition I've placed in this book, hopefully you've noticed that I've stayed on top of that repetition and made clear in some way that I've been aware of it and let you know in most instances why I repeated things.

Use your own best judgment to decide how to give the proper signals to the readers to keep them engaged and help them know that you know what you're doing by allowing any repetition to stay in your work. That is what's called *planned repetition,* and it's intentional repetition with a purpose.

Chapter 25

Emphasis: ALL CAPS, *Italics*, and !!!

LET'S BE CLEAR on this; I'm not an enemy of added emphasis in writing. And in fact, some people can probably criticize me at times for using more than they would like. But as an editor I sometimes deal with writers adding *too much* emphasis or using it at the wrong time. So let's talk about that.

Some writers I've edited have added *a little too much emphasis to words and statements*!! And others have *added* WAY, WAY, TOO MUCH!!!! (Yes, I'm exaggerating—some).

Even when it comes to writing, I tend to want to view myself as being in tune with the words of Ecclesiastes 3:1.[9] There does seem to be a time for everything we deal with in life. I acknowledged in Chapter 24 that even though repetition is almost always bad in writing, there *is* a place for it as long as it's handled properly. And there's a place for added emphasis, too, as long as it's also handled properly.

Words in ALL CAPS

Generally speaking, the use of all caps for adding emphasis should be very limited in our writing. One reason for that is because it has a tendency to come across as over-emotional.

---

9 "For everything there is a season, a time for every activity under heaven" (Ecclesiastes 3:1).

And as many who communicate on social media will tell us, words in ALL CAPS often come across as YELLING.

But depending on the style employed in your work, and depending on context, as long as words formatted in all caps are used infrequently for emphasizing words—and used much less than italics—they can be read as merely stronger, special emphasis without the screaming component.

When editing, I'll allow an occasional use of words in all caps to stay, and I'll even add all caps myself occasionally if it just seems right. And to me, *seeming right* isn't just based on how I feel (i.e., my own emotions); it's based on whether or not I believe the reader will both understand and accept my feeling as natural in the context of my narrative.

Using Italics for Emphasis

Here are my basic rules for using italics, particularly in Christian writing. And my use of this style in my own work and the work of those I've edited has been accepted by editors and publishers.

Italics for Scriptures

As I mentioned earlier, whether placed within in-line quotations or block quotations, format all Scripture quotations in italics. This is not necessarily a publisher's rule; it's my rule as an editor. And I have a good reason for it.

> If Scripture quotations are consistently italicized (and if other italics are applied sparingly), emphasis provided by italics helps readers immediately recognize Scripture quotations and elevates the importance of the words of the Bible.

Once the reader recognizes that all Scripture quotations are italicized—and other quotations are not—it provides a quick, useful, and effective separation between quotations from Scripture and other quotations.

Italics for Colloquialisms, Slang, or Figures of Speech

I often use italics here and there to draw attention to colloquialisms, slang, or figures of speech. This is usually not done on long phrases—primarily only on individual words or very short phrases.

Occasionally italicizing words like these lets the reader know the writer purposely used the words and realizes they're not necessarily going to be understood by a foreign learner of English. If questioned, the added emphasis at least lets the reader know the word or words being used wasn't a mistake, and uninformed readers can always research the usage elsewhere.

Italics for Creative Wording

A writer will sometimes use creative license to make up words that won't be found in a dictionary. Words may be combined with other words; additional syllables may be added, or even a nonsensical word can be pulled out of thin air to suit the writer's purpose.

When they're used, it can be good to use italics on them to let the reader know the spelling or word usage is intentional. (I'm not addressing fantasy writing here.) Italics can also be used to signal sarcasm, poke fun at something or someone, or just to be humorous or light-hearted.

Italics for General Emphasis

As already mentioned, a writer doesn't have the ease of a speaker when relaying demeanor, emotion, or tone to a reader. Writers can't use slight inflections of the voice, facial expressions, or body language to add a feeling or special understanding to a word or phrase. So it's sometimes handy to use italics for that purpose.

Here are some examples of what I mean.

It's sometimes helpful to use italics to relay the writer's feelings to the reader.

Example:

Nobody else can do what God created *you* to do.

And it's sometimes effective to use italics on repeated words to demonstrate their relationship and tie thoughts together with pointed emphasis.

Example:

"I remember being about four years old when I felt like "someone" was with me and was watching over me. I also knew, even as a little girl, that the *someone* was God."[10]

Italics by Rule

Beyond preferences, there are guidelines for using italics in certain circumstances. Guidelines for the use of italics are included in style manuals—like *The Chicago Manual of Style*—and style manuals contain a lot more detail than I'm including here.

---

10   From *All My Hope: A Prisoner No More*, by Julie Seals, published 2023 by Bridge-Logos, pg. 8.

If you perform a search on the internet, you can find lots of opinions on this subject. And I'm adding some of mine in the following. This isn't an exhaustive list of guidelines, but it's enough to help you deal with a lot of situations.

1. Italicize the titles of all written works, including books, magazines, and newspapers.

   But use quotation marks to denote the titles of articles within them.

   Example:

   > *Her Calling: A Woman's Guide to Fulfilling Her God-given Destiny*, by Dr. Jamie Morgan, is a must-read by any woman called into ministry. And I feel like Chapter 2, "Identifying Your Calling," will be particularly helpful to many.

2. Italicize the titles of Plays, Movies, TV Programs, Radio Programs, and Podcasts.

   But use quotation marks to denote acts in a play or movie and episodes of programs.

3. Italicize the titles of Music Albums, Operas, and long musical compositions.

   But use quotation marks to denote the titles of songs in the album, acts in the opera, or movements in long musical compositions.

4. Italicize works of art.

Italicize works of art such as the painting, *The Last Supper*, by Leonardo Da Vinci, and the statue, *David*, by Michelangelo.

5. Italicize foreign words, or their translated equivalents when referring to their foreign roots, such as words used in explaining the meanings of words in Greek and Hebrew.

    Example:

    > "The word *anoint,* in the Greek language, means to pour, rub, or smear oil on someone."[11]

6. Italicize words that are not being used in their normal way but are being referenced or written about.

    Example:

    > When it comes to *Christian,* one has to wonder these days if the majority of people actually know what that means in a truly biblical sense. And what exactly is meant by both *faith* and *service*?

7. Italicize the letters of the alphabet when they're being referred to as letters.

    Example:

    > It's spelled with a lowercase *a.* That word begins with a capital *W.* That word is spelled with two

---

11   From *Her Calling: A Woman's Guide to Fulfilling Her God-given Destiny*, by Dr. Jamie Morgan, published 2023 by Bridge-Logos, pg. 153.

s's, and it ends in *e*. You know what they say about the three *R*s?

Note 1: See above that it's usually OK to use an "apostrophe s" (as in *s*'s) to denote plurals of letters. This is allowed to avoid confusion when reading. Also note above that neither the apostrophe nor the following *s* is italicized (in "two *s*'s"). And in the final sentence of the example, you'll see that when using a capitalized letter, the apostrophe isn't normally used.

Note 2: Letters used in music notation (notes and keys) are always capitalized and not italicized (e.g., "It was played in the key of C"). And letters used in describing shapes are capitalized and not italicized (e.g., L-shaped room or an S curve).

8. Italicize the first occurrence of a word when speaking of it, but don't italicize the next occurrence.

   Example:

   > *Dedication* is undervalued. It takes dedication to not only start a difficult task but also to complete it.

   Note: This works great when there are no complications of dealing with the word several times. Do what makes sense in longer passages. But however you handle this, just try to be consistent.

9. Italics can be applied to words or phrases within quotations for emphasis. But anytime that's done, the writer must acknowledge adding the emphasis. Here are two examples of adding emphasis in quotations along with examples of the writer's acknowledgments.

> Example: (Non-Scripture Block Quotation using italics for emphasis)

>> It really mattered not that the man was *willing* to do as he was instructed. After all, it was *his duty*. He had a job to do, and that job carried with it several important responsibilities, the greatest of which was his responsibility to be *faithful* to God.[99] [italics added]

> Example: (Block Quotation of Scripture using bold font for emphasis instead of italics since the Scripture is already italicized)

>> *. . . but I focus on this one thing:* **Forgetting the past** *and looking forward to what lies ahead, I* **press on** *to reach the end of the race and receive the heavenly prize for which God, through Christ Jesus, is calling us.*
>> (Philippians 3:13–14 [emphasis mine])

The Overuse of Italics

Here's my general *rule of thumb* when it comes to using italics:

Other than when applying italics by rule (and for Scripture quotations), italics—like all forms of added emphasis—shouldn't be overused. The overuse of any form of added emphasis can become clutter, become overly prominent on a page, and either rob clarity and strength from the author's thoughts or lessen the effectiveness of the desired emphasis.

Using !!! for Emphasis

I purposely wrote "!!!" in the title instead of "Exclamation Points." That's my attempt to make a visual and hopefully more effective point. And that point is to address the unconscious (or at least hopefully unconscious) tendency of some writers to allow casual forms of writing used on social media to spill over into serious writing.

Some writers who love to communicate on social media (and I'm not saying you shouldn't) seem to feel that nearly everything that's said (or rather, written, to emulate speech) should reflect an air of excitement. So some people will place exclamation points at the end of far too many sentences.

Since that's so often the case, when the writer then needs to indicate more excitement, the next sentence will end with TWO exclamation points!! Then as the emotion continues to build, the writer has to use three!!! BUT, it's REALLY important that you understand my feelings on THIS!!!! SO, by the time I end my thoughts I want you to know I'm really REEEEEALLY EXCITED!!!!!!!!!!!

OK, I also demonstrated the overuse of ALL CAPS while making my point on the overuse of exclamation points. That was fun since I've always restrained myself from writing like that even on social media.

I now see the appeal.

But imagine if you were presented an entire book written in a social-media style. After starting to read a book written in a style like that, how many readers would likely finish the book? I'm just wondering, here. Perhaps a few would, but do most authors go to the trouble and hard work of writing an entire book for a few people?

Do authors want to write only for their social media *friends* or *followers*? Is that the normal extent of the interests of most Christian writers? I say, probably not. I assume Christian authors have a much larger vision.

Let me be clear; I'm not a complete *stick-in-the-mud* when it comes to the creative use of writing and forms of emphasis. I'm not even saying a writer has to follow every one of the rules of grammar. I'm not saying a sentence should never end with three exclamation points. I'm not even saying no sentence should ever end with a word in all caps followed by an exclamation point.

I've either done it myself or allowed it to pass in a manuscript I've edited.

As I've mentioned before, there's a time and a place for just about everything. I'm only suggesting that any serious writer should consider the downside of the overuse of all forms of emphasis. There's a price to pay if you use too much added emphasis, and that extends to not just the overuse of ALL CAPS and *Italics*. That also goes for the overuse of !!!

Following is something I share with writers.

If Everything Is Emphasized . . .

I managed a department at Oklahoma State University for several years prior to my retirement after 28 years there. And during my time in management, I sometimes needed to remind some of the members of my staff that "if everything is an emergency, nothing is an emergency." And I apply a similar sentiment to adding emphasis in writing.

> When it comes to writing, if everything is emphasized, nothing is emphasized.

Of course I'm exaggerating when talking about "everything," but you should get the idea.

The point is, if words are too often emphasized using *any* of the methods I addressed above, many readers will begin ignoring the emphasis and just start viewing the writer as either overly emotional or inexperienced. Any form of emphasis should be applied carefully and sparingly, or it will lose its effect.

A writer should by default add the least amount of emphasis necessary in both the number of occurrences and in the tone of the emphasis. That will make the emphasis that *is* added more effective.

And if a writer methodically makes it a practice to first turn to using italics to draw *occasional* special attention to words, when a word or two here and there are then formatted with all caps, that emphasis will mean more to the reader.

And applying the same reasoning to the use of exclamation points, a writer should be careful not to use too many of them. An exclamation point should not be placed on sentence after sentence in a paragraph. And consecutive paragraphs should rarely end with exclamation points.

An exclamation point, like all other forms of emphasis, loses value in any serious writing when used too often. If everything is an exclamation, nothing is an exclamation.

Tense

IT'S IMPORTANT FOR writers to choose proper verbs to relay their thoughts to the reader. And it's important for writers to have a good grasp on the proper conjugation of those verbs. But dealing with all the possible conjugations of verbs is outside the scope of this book.

The focus of our dealing with verb conjugation, here, is to focus merely on maintaining a proper tense when writing and to hit on some general things that will help an author write more clearly and accurately for the benefit of the reader.

Staying Put in Time

It's the writer's responsibility to keep the reader's mind in the proper time frame. That is, we must help the reader keep up with us if we switch from talking about something that happened in the past to talking about something that's happening now—and vice versa. That means we need to be consistent with our use of present and past verb forms.

Even a small slipup in maintaining consistency in the use of present and past tenses can confuse the reader. So if you're writing in present tense, keep the reader's mind in the present. Choose verb conjugations carefully to keep the reader's mind there. And if you're writing in past tense, consistently use verbs in past tense to keep the reader's mind focused on the past events until it's clearly time to bring the reader back to the present.

> Be careful not to jerk the reader's mind back and forth in time for no good reason, and make sure you don't leave any room for the reader to think you might be confused when it comes to the difference between present and past tenses of verbs.

The Perfect Tenses

While the use of the *perfect tenses* of verbs is important when required, my recommendation to authors is to consistently avoid both the present perfect and the past perfect tenses unless they're absolutely needed.

The use of the perfect tenses can complicate writing and make reading more difficult than it needs to be. Again, the perfect tenses certainly should be used when necessary, but when they're not needed, avoid them.

Organized below are examples of common conjugations within *Present Tense* and *Past Tense*.

Present Tenses

Tense	Example 1	Example 2
Simple Present:	I go	He drives
Present Progressive:	I am going	He is driving
Present Perfect:	I have gone	He has driven
Present Perfect Progressive:	I have been going	He has been driving

Look at the *Present Perfect* tense examples and take note that it can sometimes be confusing. And that's because "gone" and "driven" can be seen as past tense—even though when used in present perfect tense their primary focus is not on the past.

To *go*, or to be *going*, clearly speaks of something either happening now or something that's "going" to happen in the future. But the use of "gone" isn't so clear, especially combined with the word "have."

All I can say is, "That's English for you!"

The word "have" itself sounds like it could belong in past tense. And the combination of the two words definitely can cause the mind to focus on an action in the past. But while "I have gone," or "He has driven" may indeed speak in part of the past, their main focus is on the present. <u>The Present Perfect tense is called *present perfect* because although it refers to something that started in the past, the action is continuing in the present.</u>

While the present perfect tense definitely has its place—that is, it can be needed and even required when its use is grammatically correct—sometimes people use present perfect habitually even when it's either grammatically wrong or unnecessary. So it can be a little difficult to handle compared to the other present tenses, and its overuse can make reading more difficult than it has to be.

> Use the *Present Perfect* tense as needed,
> but if it isn't needed, consider
> rewriting the sentence.

Example—written with present perfect:

> "Do you go to church every Sunday?" he asked.
>
> "Yes, I have gone to church all my life."

Example—written with simple present:

> "Do you go to church every Sunday?" he asked.
>
> "Yes, I do."

In the above examples, the present perfect tense was used first to answer the question. In the second example, simple present was used. Both answered the question, but which one was easier to read? Definitely the second one.

While the answer in the first example gave us additional information (the person not only attends church now but also did in the past), the writer should decide if that information is so necessary to merit making the reading more difficult.

The simple three-word sentence, "Yes, I do," does a fine job of answering the question. But the writer could also write only, *Yes*, to make the reading even easier. The simple present was less wordy and answered the original question. But if the writer really wants the reader to know about the person's historical church attendance, by all means the writer needs to use present perfect.

Past Tenses

Tense	Example 1	Example 2
Simple Past:	I went	He drove
Past Progressive:	I was going	He was driving
Past Perfect:	I had gone	He had driven
Past Perfect Progressive:	I had been going	He had been driving

When it comes to *Past Perfect*, it's sometimes also difficult to understand or apply—but not necessarily in the same way as the present perfect. There's a relationship between the past perfect and present perfect, but it's with a twist.

Although the word "had" can function as a simple past conjugation of the verb "have," as in "I had a headache," it has a different personality altogether when it comes to being combined with another verb and used in a sentence that already speaks of the past.

> The Past Perfect form of a verb is used to relate to something that's not simply in the past. The past perfect refers to something that happened at least one more step farther in the past.

Example:

> *Then all his servants passed before him; and all the Cherethites, all the Pelethites, and all the Gittites, six hundred men who had followed him from Gath, passed before the king.*
>
> (2 Samuel 15:18 NKJV)

In the above example, the entire sentence speaks of a past event. In the sentence we read of six hundred men who passed before the king. And those were men who followed him from Gath. But the use of the past perfect tense with "who *had* followed" adds more information for us.

The writer's use of the past perfect, "had followed," makes clear to us that the six hundred men had *already* followed the king from Gath sometime *before* they passed before him.

They didn't just pass before the king *as* they followed the king from Gath. They indeed passed before the king in the past (from the perspective of the author), and they followed the king from Gath even prior to that—one step farther in the past.

To be clear then—and also somewhat repetitive—the use of the past perfect tense in this case gave us additional information and clarified the timing of past events that we could have or would have otherwise missed. So when properly employed, the past perfect tense is helpful.

But there are those who use past perfect tense *a lot.* And some of that use is not needed for clarity. There's disagreement among some writers about how often past perfect should be used. I stand with that segment of writers who believe it should be avoided anytime it's possible without causing confusion or misunderstanding.

> While the past perfect tense is indeed helpful in many instances, I suggest you refrain from using it unless it's absolutely needed to make your writing clearer and add value to your narrative.

Also take note that the constant use of the past perfect tense not only makes reading more difficult, it often makes the style feel formal, old, and stiff.

I once read a comment by someone on a discussion list who seemed to think writers should use the past perfect tense as often as they can. And by his writing I could see that he found great satisfaction in not only proving he had mastered the past perfect tense but also in promoting its use anytime writers could find an opportunity to slip it into their sentences.

I agree with many others who say the past perfect tense should only be used when it's necessary to *clarify the order of past events* for the reader (so the reader doesn't get confused). If there's no opening in your writing for the reader to get confused about what happened in the proper order in the past, there's no reason to use the past perfect conjugation.

Use simple past if simple past provides enough understanding and clarity to your narrative.

— Chapter 27 —

Voice

THIS CHAPTER IS not about "finding your voice." When people speak of *finding your voice* they're talking about writers discovering the best manner in which to present themselves in their writing. They talk about the particular niche they'll fill in writing or the style they'll ultimately be known for.

We should always attempt to improve our writing skills, but I don't think we need to spend too much time—especially in the beginning of our journey in writing—being involved in some kind of mystical process of *finding* our voices. Over time we'll develop into the writers we'll become.

If God is calling you to write, just start writing. Use whatever voice and skills you have. Give them to God for Him to use, and as you do that, your voice and skills will develop and mature over time.

Be yourself. Be vulnerable and let people know who you are. People don't want to know who you aren't. Let your readers get to know *you*—not the world-famous orator or writer you may be tempted to want to emulate.

If you're not an expert in theology, don't try to write like one. If you've never been a parent, don't write like the ultimate authority on parenting. If you're Paul, don't write like you're Peter. If you're Martha, don't write like you're Mary. Write like *you* and share what YOU have to share.

You're the one with a story to tell, and you should be the one to tell it. You're the one called to write for the benefit of those in whatever section of society or culture you have been called to reach. If God has placed a burden on you to write, that burden is yours. And He is calling you to use *your voice* to fulfill your mission.

Present all you have to God and write. Just be yourself and write with an attitude of becoming a better communicator. And with that, I lead you to what this chapter is *really* about —dealing with the Active and Passive Voices.

The Difference Between Two Voices

I found a good explanation of the difference between writing in active or passive voice on *The Writing Center* web site of George Mason University. I don't think you'll find a better explanation.

> In a sentence, main verbs can be in active or passive voice. A main verb is ***active*** when the subject of the sentence is the ***doer*** (or the ***agent***) of the action. A main verb is ***passive*** when the subject of the sentence is the ***receiver*** of the action. In passive voice, the verb is composed of a form of "to be" (e.g., *is, is being, was, will be*) + the past participle form of the verb (e.g., *watched, stolen, made, seen*).[12]

I'm giving you the following examples to help us understand this better.

---

12   https://writingcenter.gmu.edu/writing-resources/grammar-style/active-and-passive-voice, accessed in February 2023.

Active Voice

Example of active voice:

Then some Jews arrived from Antioch and Iconium and won the crowds to their side. They stoned Paul and dragged him out of town, thinking he was dead.
(Acts 14:19)

Note in the above example of a narrative written in *active voice* that the wording is very straightforward and easy to both read and understand. The order of words (syntax) in the message is very simple. But that would not be the case if Luke had written this account in a passive voice.

Passive Voice

If I were to rewrite the Scripture above in a passive voice, it might look something like the following.

Example of passive voice:

Then Paul was stoned and dragged out of town by some Jews who arrived from Antioch and Iconium and won the crowds over to their side. He was left there by them, thinking he was dead.

There's nothing wrong with this rewrite from a grammatical standpoint. But notice how much more difficult it is to read. It's more wordy, and clearly you can tell a difference in the *voice* or manner of communicating.

The two versions provide to the reader the same basic information. But while the first version (the one actually in Scripture) consists of 28 words, my rewritten version in passive voice contains 36. It takes longer to read, and it's not as simple and straightforward to understand.

Needless to say, I won't be offering my passive version of Acts 14:19 to Bible translators anytime soon. But the truth is, as far as grammar and the message delivered to the reader are concerned, the difference between them is merely a matter of style.

Contrary to what some people believe, the use of passive voice breaks no rules of grammar. I can follow the rules of grammar and produce a work in either passive voice or active voice. So the question of which of the two I choose to employ in my writing comes down to preference.

However, as writers we should understand that we have an obligation to the readers. If we want to communicate to the readers effectively, we need to communicate in a style that our identified readership will be happier to accept. And we need to communicate clearly and succinctly in whatever style that is.

All that said, I absolutely do hold to the opinion that for most work, we're better off writing in Active Voice and departing from it only when necessary.

> Focus on writing in Active Voice as much as possible. Its simpler wording is easier to read and understand.

— Chapter 28 —

Tools

TO COMPLETE MY work on updating the language of *The Pilgrim's Progress* back in the 90s, I spent many long hours over several years in a public library researching the use of words. One of the greatest resources for that was the *Oxford English Dictionary*. It consists of several large volumes.

The Oxford English Dictionary (OED) was invaluable to me because of the details devoted to the history of each word's development and how the meaning and use of the words have changed over time. I remember wishing I had the money to purchase the volumes so I could have them in my own library and do my research from home. But that was out of the question.

Today the OED is available to anyone through the Web by subscription. Boy oh boy do I wish I could have had that available to me back then! It's so much easier for writers to do research today because of the explosion of information made available to us through the internet.

Even beyond specific applications developed and put on the internet as resources for writers, a simple search on a string of words typed into a search engine will deliver up to a writer an abundance of material. Type "active vs. passive in writing" into a search bar in a web browser and see what you get.

Now, taking advantage of what current technology provides to writers, I always keep at least three extra windows open on my desktop for quick access when writing and editing. They are (1) a web browser window open to a Bible Reference site, (2) a second browser session open to at least one dictionary site, and (3) the Windows Notepad application for simple text editing (patience—I'll explain that).

Online Bible Reference

I normally use Bible Gateway, https://biblegateway.com. Bible Gateway is a tremendous tool for looking up Scriptures in multiple Bible versions. In addition to looking up Scriptures by typing or pasting in Scripture references (with book, chapter, and verse), text strings can also be used to search for Scriptures. Hint: Surround text strings with quotation marks to search for exact phrases.

One of the efficient ways to use Bible Gateway (or any other web site that offers similar functionality) is to have it opened in multiple tabs in one browser window. I'll often have Bible Gateway open in multiple tabs with each tab containing a specific version of the Bible. It's then easy and quick to hop back and forth between versions.

Online Dictionary

Multiple dictionaries exist online. I use Merriam-Webster, https://www.merriam-webster.com/dictionary, most of the time as my primary dictionary reference. I also occasionally use https://dictionary.com to compare definitions or to see how another dictionary handles words. But there are others to suit your preference.

NOTE: For checking syntax or hyphenation, or for just refreshing my memory, I also sometimes perform simple web searches in a search engine by typing in words and phrases (e.g., "is timeframe hyphenated," "who vs. whom," "perfect tenses").

Notepad—A Simple and Ancient Text Editor

One problem I often encounter when receiving electronic files from writers is poor text formatting and the appearance of odd characters appearing in Scriptures and other quotations that they copied from web pages and pasted into manuscripts. The odd characters often appear as small, elevated circles between words; and they often exist where spaces should be separating words.

The poor formatting and odd characters sometimes appear because text formatting is carried over from the web page or other source into the manuscript when the text is pasted. The odd characters no doubt appear because special format coding is embedded with the text in the web page, and it's not understood and converted when copying and pasting text into the writer's word processing software.

It's both time consuming and annoying to correct bad formatting and remove unrecognized characters from a manuscript when the writer does a lot of copying and pasting from various online sources. And Christian writers use more references than many other writers.

In fact, it gets so annoying and time consuming that I've considered sending manuscripts back to authors and telling them to fix the problems before I continue work on their books. And I may still do that. But there's an easy solution to the problem if writers will simply take advantage of it. And that solution is to simply *not* introduce the formatting problem to start with.

Just keep a simple, bare-bones, ancient text editor (like Notepad) open on your desktop (minimized of course) for use at a moment's notice. When copying text from an online source, paste the text first into that old text editor, then after pasting it in, copy that same text from the simple text editor and paste it into your manuscript.

Unlike a word processor like Microsoft Word, the old, simple text editor will not even try to deal with the formatting or the extra coding characters that exist in a web page. It will simply ignore them and basically strip them out of the content. Then when the content is copied and pasted into the word processor, it will receive that simple string of *plain text* copied from Notepad and format it to match the style of the paragraph you're pasting it into.

The Mac Equivalent:

According to my source (my son-in-law—I don't use an Apple computer), "TextEdit" comes packaged with the Mac operating system. On the Mac you may need to use this extra step in TextEdit: To make sure formatting is removed from copied and pasted text, go to the menu settings and choose *Preferences > Format > Plain Text*.

— Chapter 29 —

Bible Versions
and God

IN THIS CHAPTER we'll focus on various Bible versions used within our work and provide some guidance on using pronouns to refer to God. We'll start with a short discussion on using multiple Bible versions.

Choosing a Default Bible Version

Unless your manuscript has a theme revolving around the examination of various Bible versions and making comparisons between them, you need to identify *one* version of the Bible for your default source of reference. After identifying that version you should stick to using that version in developing the vast majority of your work.

This is not just my opinion. It's a belief I share with many others, including publishers.

This doesn't mean other versions can't also be used here and there in the same manuscript, but there is a certain weakness contained in a manuscript that shows an author using many versions of the Bible while having no version basically anchoring the work.

In my opinion, with no clear version as a default, constantly hopping around from one version to another can leave an impression with the reader that the writer may be more interested in finding a Bible reference that supports what the writer wants to believe or say instead of the writer holding himself or herself to the task of *"rightly dividing the word of truth"* (2 Timothy 2:15b NKJV).

I'm talking about appearances here from a reader's perspective; I'm not making any accusations.

In sticking mainly to using the default version, there's also something to be said about demonstrating consistency and making it easier on the readers if they have an interest in looking up Scripture references for more information and context. But beyond that, there's even another advantage to having a default version.

When we establish one default version, we then write one permission statement in our book that clearly establishes that version as the default source of reference, and then we don't need to constantly place that version's abbreviation in every reference in the book. We add a version's abbreviation to a Scripture reference only when we quote from a different version.

If you examine the Scripture references I put in this book, you'll see the abbreviation of the version in the reference missing in many instances. That means the Scripture is from my default version, *The New Living Translation*. The permission statement covering that is on the permissions page inside the book's front cover. The Scripture I quoted a few paragraphs earlier is from the NKJV, so I placed that inside the reference.

Pronouns Used for God

There's some confusion these days about how to refer to God using pronouns. So this is worth talking about. To get this started, let's first look at the way the style guide most used by book publishers addresses the pronouns.

The Chicago Manual of Style actually states that pronouns referring to God should NOT be capitalized. And the reason they give for that is the fact that the pronouns referring to God in nearly all historical Bible versions are not capitalized. While there may indeed be publishers who strictly follow *The Chicago Manual* on this, it's absolutely common for both Christian publishers and writers to break from *The Chicago Manual's* recommendation by using "He, Him, and His."

Christian writers commonly capitalize these pronouns, and there are some good reasons for that. For most writers, it's a sign of respect. But for me as an editor there is actually a grammatical component to it. I've seen for a long time that the use of *He*, *Him*, and *His* has been helpful many times in clarifying for me and other readers who the "he" or "He" is—that is, which "he" the writer is referring to.

When reading the writing of others about God and His interactions with men, I've seen plenty of sentences over the years in which, if the pronoun referring to God were not capitalized, the pronoun used for God could have been read to refer to the other "he" in the narrative.

Moving on from that, consistency is always important in writing, and here is the standard I employ and ask all writers I edit to follow: Consistently capitalize *He*, *Him*, and *His* when referring to God. But don't capitalize "himself."

I ask writers not to capitalize *himself* because I believe it's visual overkill and not necessary at all. I join with those who believe it serves no purpose since the identity of "himself" should always be clearly defined by context. And keep in mind that America's leading style manual doesn't want us to capitalize *any* of the pronouns.

One thing for sure, though, if even one of the three pronouns (of he, him, and his) is capitalized, capitalize *all* of them. It makes no sense to do otherwise. And it also makes no sense at all to capitalize a pronoun referring to God the Father or God the Son without also capitalizing a pronoun referring to God the Holy Spirit.

Capitalizing You and Your

Now it's really getting interesting, for while most respected versions of the Bible don't have *any* of God's pronouns capitalized, a few newer versions do. And of course that doesn't bother me since I actually think it's a good idea to capitalize *He*, *Him*, and *His*. But an even smaller number of versions go a bit further and capitalize "You" and "Your" in passages when the original writer or character in the Scripture is speaking to God.

And capitalizing *You* and *Your* is something I personally don't like. I know, that's my problem, right? True, but it's primarily only my problem because it causes issues with sentence clarity and reading. Just as I see *Himself* as overkill and visually intrusive, *You* and *Your* make matters much worse.

Since some Bible translators and editors chose to employ the capitalization of *You* and *Your*, more writers have adopted that style. And just as I feel strongly about capitalizing *He*, *Him*, and *His*, they feel strongly about *You* and *Your*. And when I receive manuscripts from them to edit I'm forced into my bad-guy identity to do my best to talk them out of it.

To me, the worst thing about capitalizing each and every pronoun for God is that when writers decide to add a prayer to their work (and many will add more than one) there are so many occurrences of *You* and *Your* in prayers that reading becomes hard, and the focus of the eyes and mind while reading can't help from being distracted by the extra emphasis added to numerous *You's* and *Your's*.

The additional capitalized pronouns demand attention. And that can become so visually overwhelming that the author's attempt to honor and respect God takes the focus and power away from what the author is actually saying.

So for me, the reader, what's more important?

After working for several years on projects as a Civil Engineering Technician, I shifted specialties and began producing Architectural and Mechanical plans. I also did that for years. One of the things I had to learn and deal with in all that project work—regardless of specialty—was the need to not only produce accurate construction plans for projects but also draw them in such a way that they served the needs of the *readers of the plans*, who were tasked with actually doing the construction.

It was my responsibility to realize what needed to POP (a term we used) for the eyes of the reader. In the way all the details were designed and drawn, I needed to ensure that nothing important in the plans was visually covered up by something less important. And no doubt that affects my feelings about allowing *anything* to cover up or take emphasis away from an important statement or meaning in an author's work.

I discussed this with the copyeditor of a major book publisher, and he understands the problem. He talked about how even though some writers may feel obliged out of respect to capitalize all pronouns referring to God, the fact that they do doesn't prove they respect God any more than a writer who doesn't capitalize them. I agreed.

Then the copyeditor gave me some insight into how he viewed dealing with the issue, and it was something I wasn't expecting. In his work as copyeditor, he allows the capitalization of *You* and *Your* as long as *You* and *Your* are also capitalized in the default Bible version used by the author.

So if you use the *New King James Version* as your default source of reference, and if your publisher feels the same way he does, you're welcome to capitalize "You" and "Your." And if your publisher doesn't really care, capitalize the pronouns as you like. But if you find yourself working with an editor who shares my views, you might want to prepare yourself to be challenged to do otherwise.

— Chapter 30 —

Proofing

SEVERAL THINGS MOTIVATED me to produce this book. But I believe all of those things grew out of good soil made up of a mixture of primarily two ingredients. The first ingredient is my belief that, especially as Christians, it's important for all of us to do what's necessary to produce excellent work. That's what God deserves from us.

As for the second ingredient, it's my belief that God approves of His people working together and intends for us to help each other accomplish His purposes.

The Bible reveals to us there are many giftings delivered to believers, and we don't all share the same ones. But together, the Body of Christ is complete.

> Together, we're equipped to represent Christ as He desires. The Church (*capitalized*) consists of *all* believers. And since the Church is one in Him, that can only mean we're one in Him together.

With the multiple aptitudes and natural abilities of individual believers combined with individual giftings and empowerments provided to us through the Holy Spirit, we're at our best working in partnership. As partners we're at our best to fulfill our individual callings, and we're at our best to accomplish the Great Commission—together.

That's how it's meant to be.

And now getting back to the first ingredient in the good soil I mentioned above—in my attempt to work together with you, I hope I've helped you see that no Christian writer should be satisfied with presenting to God a manuscript that undersells that writer's true abilities.

Most of us find over time that we could have done better on our projects if we had tried harder and perhaps done one more thing before we declared we were done. So here's my challenge: Learn well and accept a few simple words spoken to me years ago by my own editor.

> Good writing
> is in rewriting.

The Reason for Proofing

There's no set number of times that writers should proof their work. I can't tell you how many times to go over your work and proof your completed manuscript before turning it over to an editor or presenting it to a publisher. I can't tell you to do it two times, five times, or even ten times.

I can tell you, though, that I've worked on manuscripts I wished writers would have proofed *one more time* before presenting them to me. And I've also wished that I would have proofed my own work again before turning it over to someone to review. The point is, there's a good reason for a writer to do a thorough job of proofing and re-proofing a manuscript before being satisfied with it.

No writers should get down in the dumps about their writing skills just because they make mistakes in writing or write things that need to be rewritten. We all make mistakes, and rewriting is actually part of the process of producing good writing. And I'm not saying writers should expect their work to be perfect; that will certainly kill the writer's desire to write. I'm only saying writers should **not** be satisfied with anything less than the best they can do.

God doesn't expect everything we do to be perfect in our eyes or in the eyes of others; we're only complete in Him! But I strongly believe God expects us to refuse to satisfy ourselves with mediocrity. There are massive loads of *Mediocrity* being pulled in trailers behind the multitudes who are driving down the wide and accommodating road to destruction. Reaching mediocrity in our work takes little to no effort.

> *You can enter God's Kingdom only through the narrow gate. The highway to hell is broad, and its gate is wide for the many who choose that way. But the gateway to life is very narrow and the road is difficult, and only a few ever find it.* (Matthew 7:13-14)

This passage of Scripture speaks of salvation, but I believe within it is also a principle about dealing with difficulty.

Choose the difficult road that leads toward excellence, even in your writing. If you strive for excellence in what you do, God will instruct you through the work of the Holy Spirit and provide to you the knowledge and abilities you need to improve every facet of your existence in Him, including your writing skills.

> The need to give your best to Jesus is the most important reason I can give you for thoroughly proofing your work and even rewriting it again and again if necessary.

The Mechanics

In my experience as an editor, if I were to name only one general thing that more writers could do in order to increase their abilities to proof and improve their work prior to submitting it to others, it's to employ some basic *mechanics*.

When it comes to *mechanics*, you may wonder what I'm talking about. Well, what I'm really addressing here is the willingness and determination of writers to go through the intentional, conscious, and physical process of looking for, identifying, and fixing problems.

For instance, in the past I've advised writers to physically make a list of some of the problems that repeatedly show up in their writing. Then I tell them they should read through it as a checklist, point by point, and go through their manuscript to find and fix problems when proofing.

Doing that is not part of the creative process of writing; it's mechanical. For instance, if I'm really bad about not putting a comma before every coordinating conjunction that connects two independent clauses, I can use the search mechanism in my word processor to search for every "and" or "but" in the manuscript and examine the relationship between clauses joined by them. (Search for other common conjunctions as well.)

Does that take time? Of course! What can I say? But if I take the time now to routinely look for repeated issues in my writing, I'll be more apt to learn and not have to deal with the issues so much in the future. And if I take the time to do it, my editor won't; and that may even save me some money.

If I have a tendency to use the old typewriter method of spacing sentences and put two spaces between them instead of allowing modern word processing software to take care of sentence spacing, I can perform a search and fix every occurrence of two spaces in the manuscript. I can replace every occurrence of two spaces with one space in the entire document by pressing only a few keys on the keyboard.

If I inserted an extra carriage return between paragraphs instead of allowing paragraph styles in my document to take care of spacing between paragraphs, I can find those and delete them. Then the editor also won't have to deal with that.

If I have a problem with the capitalization of certain words, I can search for those words with case-matching enabled and fix those. If I have a problem with the repetitive use of any word, I can perform a search for every occurrence of that word and see how I did on rewording or using synonyms to keep from repeating the same word over and over.

But of course, my thoughts on the mechanics of writing and proofing go further than what we can do with software. It even extends to the idea that we lay down our work for several days and return later to proof it with fresher eyes. With fresher eyes and clearer minds, we can read our valuable statements again and consciously find the problems that may kill them.

The few things I've mentioned here in what you may view as a closing rant on my part is only part of our work of proofing and improving our writing. And I'm certainly talking about WORK. Writing is not easy work. But it's work worth doing if your goal is to bless your readers with the wonderful things God wants you to share with them.

The Paper Proof

When it comes to your initial proofing, I assume you'll do that electronically in your word processing software. At least that's the way I do it. I write, edit, read and re-read, proof, rewrite, edit, and proof again several times on the computer before I'm satisfied at all with my work.

But eventually—once you think your manuscript is complete—you should print it out to read on paper. I can't explain this scientifically, but I know when we read our writing on paper, our eyes will see things we didn't see or couldn't recognize as problems on the computer screen.

On this very book, my manuscript was at a point where I was pretty satisfied with it. It looked ready to go. Then I printed it out on paper. And when I read it on paper some things began jumping out to me that needed to be improved. I saw problems with tone here and there. I recognized some sentences that needed to be improved for reading. I recognized some things that just really didn't need to be said.

I put marks and wrote things all over that paper copy. Then I went about modifying the manuscript based on those mark-ups. And *strangely*, as I made those modifications I even saw the need to modify some of them further as I read over the changes I made on screen.

I used the word, "strangely." Actually, that was sarcastic. It wasn't strange at all, and that's part of my point in emphasizing to you the importance of reading your manuscript on paper and proofing your work again and again.

After going through that process, I did it all over again. Once again I printed the entire manuscript on paper and repeated the process. Hopefully you're a better writer than I am and won't have to work so hard.

— Chapter 31 —

Graduating from Boot Camp

IT'S NOT POSSIBLE for me to forget the cold winter of 1972 as I shivered and suffered my way through Basic Training, the U.S. Army's version of Boot Camp, at Fort Leonard Wood, Missouri. Those were some of the more miserable months in my life. There were hard lessons to learn about life outside of the comfortable confines of home.

I've lost memories over the years about some of my experiences in life, but still vivid in my mind is looking out of the window and gazing at the entry of the army base as the bus I was riding in drove through the main gate of Fort Leonard Wood. As I read the name of the training base at the gate, I had a foreboding, deep feeling that my world was suddenly changing, and there was nothing I could do to turn back.

I and my fellow recruits filed out of the bus, and our education in being a soldier began. We learned rather quickly that we were no longer in charge of our lives. Our freedom to go where we wanted to go, and our freedom to do what we wanted to do, were taken from us. We learned right away that when we put on our new uniforms we were not our own.

We were no longer in charge—of anything.

We did only what we were told to do. We were told where to sleep. We were told when to go to bed. We were told when to wake up. We were told when to eat. We were told when to walk. We were told when to run. We were told when to stand. We were told when to work. We were told when to rest. And we were told how far we could go from our barracks.

For the first few weeks of training, we couldn't even step off the curb directly behind our barracks to walk across the street to buy a can of soda from a vending machine. But there was a purpose for all the rules and demands. Those in charge were teaching us things that could be learned no other way.

There were things to learn beyond the various skills of a warrior and how to obey orders. For instance, I learned I could survive challenge and hardship. I learned a great deal about camaraderie and how it often takes working together with others to accomplish important things. And I learned that strong ties are formed when people have to pull together to survive.

The call to serve one's country is a call to sacrifice. And when some answer that call, they give up their very lives in service. There's no higher calling than for men and women to lay down their lives for the good of others. And Jesus answered such a call.

The plan was drawn. The call was clear. And it echoed throughout the Universe. The call rang out for the *only one who could* to step forward and make the ultimate sacrifice of service. Jesus, who lived in such glory that He took part in creating or making possible everything we have ever known, answered that call. He agreed to leave His place in heaven and lower himself to live an earthly existence.

When Jesus arrived at His destination, He became dependent on others to give Him anything and everything He needed to allow Him to survive. And as He grew as a child and into adulthood, He learned by experience what it meant to not only depend on others but also obey those in authority over Him.[13] Then when the time came for Him to obey and fulfill His calling, He gave His life to save us.

Jesus gave all He had to give. And God is surely calling you now to give what *you* have. In answering the call that your spiritual ears now hear, you too will learn by experience. You'll move from experience to experience as you learn more and more about how you fit into God's plan for your life.

Much is ahead of you as you follow your calling. There will be challenges and likely hardships you can't now anticipate. But have no fear, your training will prepare you for dealing with those things.

You've gone through the gate. There's no turning back. Your life is not your own. Your service belongs to God. And He has set over you the ultimate trainer in the person of the Holy Spirit. He will guide you into all truth. He will teach you what you need to know. And through Him, God will impart to you the tools you'll need to fulfill your calling.

When you graduate from boot camp, you'll know so much more than you knew before. You'll be well prepared to do the things you're called upon to do, and you'll be able to do them better than you ever thought possible.

---

13   "Even though Jesus was God's Son, he learned obedience from the things he suffered" (Hebrews 5:8).

Closing

If there's even one thing, one aspect of writing, that I've helped you with by putting together this book, then as far as I'm concerned, my effort was worth it. And as you write, if you feel this book has in any way better equipped you to fulfill the Great Commission, then I'm both thrilled and humbled that God would allow me to partner with you in that task.

> Be a Great Commission writer.
> Christian writers have the honor of serving others by sharing with them the timeless message of salvation.

God has given each of you a gift from his great variety of spiritual gifts. Use them well to serve one another. Do you have the gift of speaking? Then speak as though God himself were speaking through you. Do you have the gift of helping others? Do it with all the strength and energy that God supplies. Then everything you do will bring glory to God through Jesus Christ. All glory and power to him forever and ever! Amen. (1 Peter 4:10–11)

THE JOHN BUNYAN COLLECTION

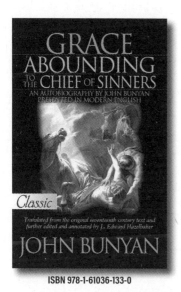

ISBN 978-1-61036-133-0

ISBN 978-0-88270-757-0

ISBN 978-1-61036-153-8

Add John Bunyan's three most popular books to your library today. Read them to appreciate the depth of Bunyan's understanding of Biblical truth and his dedication to Christian service. The language within each of these books written in the 17th century was carefully updated for today's readers by L. Edward Hazelbaker.

ALL MY HOPE
Julie Seals

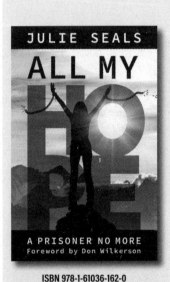

ISBN 978-1-61036-162-0

Julie knew she could spend the rest of her life in prison if she were caught crossing the border with four pounds of methamphetamine duct-taped around her waist. But life had become so overwhelming, so painful, that she no longer cared if she lived or died. So she crossed over the border. And with her arrest as a drug smuggler that day, her years of running from responsibility—and from God—came to an end. Through one miraculous event after another, God transformed Julie from drug dealer to Hope Dealer. Read her story now as Julie Seals unveils her extraordinary journey of overcoming a 17-year addiction to crystal meth and being transformed by the supernatural power of God.

JULIESEALS.COM

HER CALLING
Dr. Jamie Morgan

Her Calling is a mentor in a book. Dr. Jamie Morgan uses her decades of experience and insightful leadership to inspire women to fulfill their God-given destinies. All women called to ministry will be blessed by the practical guidance and wisdom shared by Jamie Morgan. Regardless of what God has called you to do in your ministry, this book will become one of your most valuable resources.

JAMIEMORGAN.COM

ISBN 978-1-61036-080-7